S0-BJB-084

From the book...

Presently Little Sea came out of the house dressed in a red and white pareu, and her hair, scented with coconut oil, shimmering in the moonlight. She was ready for the promenade.

I should like to describe the events of that night in detail, but for various reasons it will be best to pass lightly over them; furthermore, I was too intoxicated to remember everything clearly.

The wide outer beach sparkled beneath the moon, a couch fit for any island princess. The reef combers seemed to grumble jealously as they leaned over the coral and lost themselves in foaming phosphorescent pools in the lagoon. The water was as clear as the sky; we could see the fantastic coral shapes and their myriad colors, softened and shaded by the moonlight. We waded in—it was only waist-deep—and splashed about like four-year-old babies; and later we dried our bodies by racing along the sand, dancing, and singing. Then, lying on the beach, Little Sea pointed out the stars, told me their native names and some quaint little legends about them.

Before returning we did all kinds of foolish things; among others I taught her how to kiss in the civilized manner, for she knew only the calflike rubbing of noses and sniffing. But when she had mastered the civilized art, she in turn became teacher, giving me lessons in the native *ongi-ongi*...

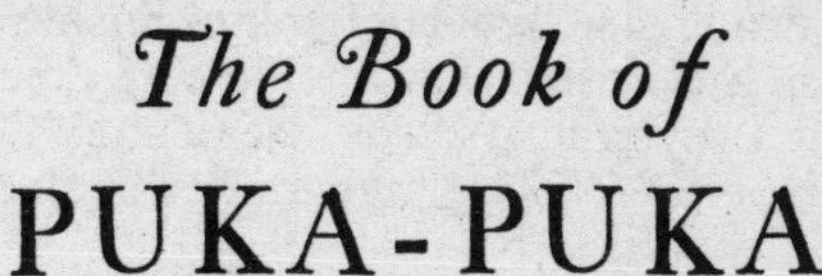

The Book of PUKA-PUKA

By

ROBERT DEAN FRISBIE

Illustrated by

MAHLON BLAINE

MUTUAL PUBLISHING

COMPANY · *Honolulu*

Copyright, 1928, by Atlantic Monthly Co. Copyright, 1928, 1929, by Century Co. Copyright renewed 1957 by Charles Mataa Frisbie, William Hopkins Frisbie, Elaine Frisbie Over, Nga Frisbie Dawson, Florence Frisbie Hebenstreit. Copyright, 1929, by The Century Co. Copyright renewed 1957 by Florence Frisbie Hebenstreit.

Copies of this book will not be imported into the United States in violation of any version of the Manufacturing Clause that might take effect before they reach the United States.

Cover painting by Jack Delaney.

Cover design by The Art Directors.

Printed in Australia by
The Book Printer, Victoria.

THIS BOOK CONTAINS THE COMPLETE TEXT OF THE ORIGINAL HARDBOUND EDITION

THESE memories of a few of my years on Puka-Puka are dedicated to the man who urged me to write them down—

JAMES NORMAN HALL

Pe toku yana wawine Puka-Puka,
Ya takere i te t'i roto;
E wu tamawine e patua e te t'i
Waka yongi-yongi toku matangi vave.

Puka-Puka resembles my mistress,
Naked in light ripples swimming;
Breaking the sea waves, a maiden breast
Hungrily wind-kisses winning.

—*From* "Mako Wenua" (*A chant of the land*).

Ropati Frisbie, South Sea Trader

His greatest dream in life was to write a book like Herman Melville's *Moby Dick*, which would tell the absolute, unveiled truth about one man's thoughts and feelings. As a means to this end, to attain the solitude required for such a task, he would build himself a "little boat," broad in beam and thirty-six feet over all.

He explained his goal to James Norman Hall, another American writer who had settled in Tahiti only a few months earlier and who had met Robert Dean Frisbie at the steamer landing one day in 1920. Frisbie came ashore with a portable typewriter in one hand and a camera in the other, and gazed with delight along the sea wall. Over the green pathway projected the sterns of moored small craft—island schooners laden with oily copra, fishing vessels, yachts of wealthy globetrotters.

"I suppose one could go anywhere from here," he told his new friend. "I could load my boat with trade goods and sail from island to island, making enough to live on and writing out my ponderings, the way old Montaigne did in his French castle."

Over lunch at the Hotel Tiare began a friendship that was to last throughout the newcomer's lifetime. Hall learned then and later about Frisbie's earlier life and hopes.

Robert Dean Frisbie had been born in Cleveland, Ohio, in 1896, younger son of Arthur Grazly Frisbie and Florence Benson of Vermont. The father was a weak dreamer brought up as a Quaker, but sought further reassurance in one or another group, such as the Theosophists, the Christian Scientists, and the Order of the Magi. When Robert was twelve, he and his brother Charles began four years in a rather monastic school at Point Loma, California, where they rose at six o'clock, suffered a vigorous military drill before breakfast, and then, as at all other meals, ate in silence. They were not allowed to read newspapers or learn anything of the rest of the world except for two hours a week, when they could visit their parents. Robert was a thin, frail child, devoted all his life to his mother; he took refuge in voracious reading and secret writing of verses. He read everything he could find about the South Seas; Robert Louis Stevenson was his idol. He was continually rebellious against the rigid discipline at Point Loma, and increasingly determined to leave America.

After holding various jobs, young Frisbie enlisted in the United States Army toward the end of World War I. Life in the 8th Cavalry in a Texas training camp did nothing to improve his tendency toward tuberculosis. At his last medical examination in the Army the doctor reportedly told him that he would not be able to live out another winter in America. He was medically discharged in 1918 with a monthly pension of $45—a sum that in his later years might make the difference between mere existence and near-starvation on a South Sea atoll.

Frisbie told Hall that he hoped this pension, supplemented by selling photographs and articles to a newspaper syndicate, would enable him to build his boat and allow him leisure to write the great book that would make him famous. He could not afford to fail. Hall, himself something of a dreamer, was tempted to say that any man who believed he could tell the complete truth about himself had a fatal defect of vision to start with, but it seemed likely that this young man would soon discover it for himself.

Frisbie began with zest the role of beachcomber. Within a year he bought a four-acre plantation at Papeari, about thirty miles around the coast from the main town of Papeete, and there built himself a native-style house of bamboo, thatched with woven palm fronds. His neighbors were simple Polynesian folk who liked Robert, or "Ropati," as Frisbie was usually called during the rest of his life. He quickly learned their language and tried to escape "civilization" by sharing their routines.

Most of his time, then and later, was spent gathering and consuming the great books of the world that he hoped would make up for his cult-tainted lack of education. He ordered many through his brother Charles, and during the years he somehow accumulated two hundred volumes: Montaigne, Swinburne, George Borrow, Francois Villon's poems, Dante, the travels of Mungo Park, George Meredith's novels, and the essays of Lamb and especially De Quincey. Reading in his leafy hideaway, with his lovely Tahitian mistress Terii by his side, he could easily pass three years as if in a dream of faerie.

On his rare visits to Papeete, however, the man of solitude became a different person. Sensitive to the comments of other foreign residents of the French possession, who felt that his "going native" reflected on their own codes of behavior, Ropati would gulp down two rum punches and soon become the brawling, boasting beachcomber of legend.

Frisbie did find time to travel from Papeete. He sailed to the neighboring Paumotu group, the "Dangerous Archipelago"; encountered a waterspout and a tidal wave; and dived for pearls with the Society Islanders of Hikueru. And back at Papeari, he fell in love with a thirty-foot yawl called the *Motuovini*. In partnership with two other penniless residents who yearned to sail to far islands, he began the exhausting task of rebuilding the yacht for ocean voyaging.

Trouble besieged Ropati and his partners, E.J. Spies and R.A. Sampson. By February, 1923, the adventurers had sunk two thousand dollars into the refitting of the yawl and still would have to buy her sails and all their provisions for a planned fourteen-month cruise, meanwhile starving themselves to dangerous slenderness in order to put every penny into the task. Robert received no encouragement from his father, who wrote that he was praying that the proposed voyage would not happen.

Finally, on a June morning, the three voyagers proudly hauled up the French tricolor and made ready to sail. The yawl's deck was heaped with bunches of green bananas, drinking coconuts, yams, dried fish and clams, and cases of rum. It was also jammed with a crowd of Tahitian friends, to whom a departure was an occasion for riotous celebration.

An even wilder occasion was the reception of the yacht at the atoll of Manihiki, about nine hundred miles northeast of Tahiti. The Americans finally tore themselves away, and three days later made landfall at Tongareva or Penrhyn Island, some two hundred and fifty miles to the northeast. The voyagers then left to explore northward, hoping to discover an uncharted equatorial isle called Victoria. They gave up the quest after two weeks and headed to the southwest for the Fiji group in black Melanesia, visiting on the way the uninhabited atoll called Suwarrow. "Buried treasure" had twice been found here, and Ropati made a note to return to this forsaken spot about six hundred miles northeast of Samoa. Almost hysterical welcomes were accorded the yachtsmen at both American and Western Samoa, and at the end of September they took refuge at the port of Suva, capital of Fiji.

The refitted yawl had sailed three thousand miles on the tumultuous Pacific, riding majestically through a ninety-mile gale and making her masters proud. But they could not live in Fiji without funds during the hurricane months, and were forced to sell the vessel and return to Tahiti.

There Ropati received the happy news that his first

magazine article, "Fei-hunting in Polynesia," had been accepted by *Forum* magazine. He left his Papeari plantation for good early in March, 1924, sailing with dashing Captain Andy Thomson on the schooner *Avarua* to Rarotonga, capital of the Cook Islands, some seven hundred miles southwest of Tahiti. At Rarotonga, headquarters of A.B. Donald & Company, began a new and different adventure for Ropati Frisbie that was to become the highest point in a life of high points in the Pacific.

Frisbie's new post was to run a trading station for A.B. Donald & Company on a small island. The duties would not be onerous; he would be able to live in tropical comfort, leaving most of his days free for writing the great book. On a small atoll in the northern part of the Cook Islands, one of the loneliest specks of land in the vast Pacific Ocean, he found a spot that would be forever after associated with his name.

Puka Puka—which got its native name from the hernandia trees growing prominently on its shores—was seen by the Spanish explorer Don Alvaro de Mendana on his 1595 voyage, and rediscovered by Captain John Byron of H.M.S. *Dolphin* on that ship's first round-the-world voyage in 1765. It was visited in 1857 by an emissary of the London Missionary Society, and six years later was raided by slavers from Peru. More than a hundred of its Polynesian inhabitants were kidnapped and taken off to toil and die in the guano mines of South America. It was annexed by Great Britain in 1892 by Captain H.W.S. Gibson of H.M.S. *Curacao*. "Danger Island," to give the place its English name, lies seven hundred and twenty miles northwest of Rarotonga, whence a supply schooner might arrive once or twice a year to carry away the copra crop, the only source of income for the six hundred people on the atoll. Ropati Frisbie could not get much farther away from civilization than Puka Puka, and he reveled in the prospect of living there for the rest of his days.

Puka Puka in the Cooks—not to be confused with another isle of that name in the Gambier group—was truly a paradise for a bachelor beachcomer. The young man from Ohio had attained the dream of millions of Americans in the post-war Twenties. He had escaped the treadmill of workaday living to the haunts of Rousseau's noble savages. He was literally the only white man on a South Sea island, surrounded by nubile, half-naked maidens whose favors were offered nightly on a moonlit beach to swains with flowers behind their ears.

Soon settled in his trading store, Frisbie began writing and sending off to New York his sketches of life on Puka Puka. All of them echoed the whispering of the trade wind in the palms and resounded with the crash of breakers on the fringing coral reef. The maidens in the moonlight were not obtrusive; in fact, several of the pieces were published in *St. Nicholas Magazine*, an established monthly for boys and girls that was to perish in the early years of the Depression. The *Atlantic Monthly* accepted most of the others. Almost thirty sketches appeared in 1929, collected by The Century Company under the title of *The Book of Puka-Puka.*

This volume, the first of half a dozen that would make Danger Island the most celebrated atoll in any ocean, was not Frisbie's *Moby Dick*, but its publication gave him courage to persist as a writer hoping for greater achievements. The book was dedicated to his Tahiti mentor, James Norman Hall, and illustrated by Mahlon Blaine, a popular woodcut artist. Each chapter was preceded by short chants in the native language, translated by the author. Its depiction of daily life on a Pacific island was filled with sweetness and light. And the national reviews were a delight to a writer far from the literary markets; a check for $50 for an article would support himself and his family for weeks. In the New York *World* Frederick O'Brien, author of four escapist books on the South Seas, wrote: "*The Book of Puka-Puka,* as the narrative of the impression of a sensitive, sensual youth in a mad environment of which he is master, and of the details of being in one of the most exotic spots in the round globe, is a first-class South Seas story. The selection of material from his vast diary is very well done, so that there is no dullness, no stupid scientific gabble by a layman, and there is little left out of real interest in the doings and sayings of the Puka-Pukans, from birth to death." Charles Nordhoff, Hall's collaborator, opined in the *Saturday Review of Literature:* "In this series of sketches, closely-knit, and drawing—with seeming random lines, stipplings, and bits of light and shadow—a picture full of art, of a life so remote from that of the world at large as to be almost unintelligible, Mr. Frisbie has shown real originality and skill. The combination of qualities that make such writing possible is rare: imagination, close observation, a feeling for beauty, and a thoroughly pagan point-of-view, are some of them. Add to these a long residence among the natives, the ability to learn a different language, and a background of education and reading few South Sea traders have, and it will be perceived that the combination is rare indeed. Mr. Frisbie's writing, done with a light touch, full of gusto and undertones of irony, suits the subject well."

Frisbie was the first white trader to open the village store for the past fourteen years, and his easygoing methods of handling sales soon made him a popular figure. When his reading and writing began to pall, he could always join in the native fishing trips, bird-catching sport, and other games, and the moonlight diversions on the beach were not neglected. But after some time Ropati decided that a wife would solve many of his problems, and he fell in love with a petite, beautiful, and devoted Polynesian girl with all the fine qualities of her heritage.

Ngatokorua was the fourth child of a native missionary who had sailed eight hundred miles in an outrigger canoe to bring the first Christian mission to Puka Puka shortly after the turn of the century. In a simple ceremony that took place on Yato Beach on the leeward side of the island, Ropati and his bride were united under the auspices of "William the Heathen," a former whaleman who was the only islander able to speak a few words of English. Frisbie's lifelong disdain for organized churches and clergymen caused him to omit inviting the bride's father, and the only witness was one of Nga's sisters. Frisbie could not have chosen a more loving and faithful wife, for Nga followed him wherever he roved and was to bare him no fewer than five handsome, half-Polynesian children.

During his first stay on Puka Puka, Frisbie lingered for four lotus-eating years. He returned to Rarotonga in 1928, and on that island his first son, Charles, was born on June 23, 1930.

Soon thereafter he made a brief trip to San Francisco. His homecoming convinced him that the South Pacific, and particularly the atoll of Puka Puka, was the best place for him to live. On the ship sailing back to Rarotonga, he wrote to his brother: "Except for the memory of you and one or two others, the whole stay in San Francisco seems like a fantastic dream—a wild nightmare of fat hangdog little men puffing as they try to work hard enough to please their raw-boned damned women."

On his return, Ropati found that, in Polynesian fashion, his firstborn had been adopted by a grandaunt, old hunchbacked Piki-Piki, who refused to give him up; and when Frisbie returned to settle in Rarotonga in 1943, his son was thirteen—almost a grown man.

After a brief excursion to Manuae Island in a venture in copra trading, Ropati and Nga embarked on a schooner heading for Tahiti. Captain Andy Thomson made the seven-hundred-mile trip in four days through a wild gale with every stitch of canvas spread. The couple settled in the mountains and Nga learned about life in Tahiti, when food could be found for five dollars a month, supplemented by tropical produce.

This was the happiest period in Ropati's life. He began writing but destroyed two imperfect autobiographical novels. He was more successful at selling magazine articles and short stories. In spite of his discouragements when the arrival of a rejection slip meant that the Frisbies would lack many comforts for a month, Ropati did not do badly in the marketplace during the competitive era of general magazine publishing. Two of his articles appeared in the popular, green-covered *American Mercury*. Most of his items were warmly accepted by the editor of the *Atlantic Monthly*, including Frisbie's first fiction sale, "The Ghost of Alexander Perks, A.B.", a tale of a haunted trading schooner that is still quite readable today. The writer's work continued to appear in the *Atlantic* through the fall of 1943, when the periodical ran a three-part essay.

More than one of his articles appeared as chapters in *My Tahiti*, an "Atlantic Monthly Press Book" published in 1937 with drawings by W. Alister Macdonald. As the author prefaced the volume, which was dedicated to his daughter Florence: "These passages, sketches, incidents, are an attempt to recapture something of the spirit of native Tahitian life as I knew it during the first three years of the nineteen-twenties." It retained much of Frisbie's early charm and humor—especially in the section relating the showing of a William S. Hart cowboy film projected on a sheet slung between two coconut trees. As the reviewer for *Books* noted: "But the book is to be welcomed not specifically for the quality of gayety or humor or even sympathy, but for a well-roundedness of experience and observation which gives the reader a sense of island life."

By this time Ropati did indeed have a daughter to whom to dedicate a volume. In the maternity ward of the hospital in Papeete, on June 19, 1932, the first of three Frisbie daughters was born. Her nickname was "Whiskey

Johnny," and thereafter she seldom went by her Christian name of Florence. Feeling greatly the absence of his son, Frisbie vowed never to be separated from Johnny, and thereafter they were seldom apart. This daughter's name appears on two volumes of family reminiscence, and to these can be referred the reader interested in the fantastic childhoods of this South Sea clan.

Soon after the birth of Johnny, the parents sailed across the tumultuous channel to the neighboring island of Moorea, where they settled at the head of beautiful Paopao Bay. Here Ropati, in a spot where food lay rotting on the ground, went into the poultry business. He started out with twenty-two Plymouth Rock chickens; soon rabbits and goats joined the homestead.

There were drawbacks to this paradise. Ropati had recurrences of earlier attacks of filarial fever, the horrifying scourge of South Sea life, which held him in bed for days at a time. He was left with an enlarged leg swollen by elephantiasis. Such swellings in this disease were caused by accumulations of larval faeces that plugged the lymph glands and in some cases produced arms and legs as big around as tree trunks. Ropati's treatment was to wrap his swollen leg tightly with bicycle tire tubing brought from Papeete; but thereafter he was never free of the threat of returning illness. The pain was alleviated by rum, and Ropati was in danger of becoming an alcoholic.

Moreover, the family was not only penniless but in debt. Sales to magazines were rare, and a collaboration with Charles Nordhoff on a book came to nothing. In October, 1933, sixteen months after the birth of Florence, her brother William Hopkins Frisbie was born on the plantation, amid chants of Tahitian neighbors. His father nicknamed him "Hardpan Jake," and Jakey he thereafter remained.

Homesick Nga hoped that her next child would be born back on her beloved atoll of Puka Puka, and in January, 1934, a chance occurred to enable a return. As an experienced navigator, Ropati was invited to sail a yawl through the Cook Islands, winding up at the end on his old home atoll. A high point on the way was a stay on the uninhabited island of Suwarrow, owned by the trading firm of A.B. Donald, and Ropati made a note to himself that this might be an even better hideaway for a writer than Matauea Point off Ko Island at Puka Puka, the place to which Frisbie now returned with his growing family.

Elaine Metua Frisbie was born in Roto Village on November 29, 1935, and early in October, 1937, Ngatokorua-i-Matauea—called Nga for short—was born. This was a good year; *My Tahiti* appeared in New York, and money came from magazine sales. Ropati began writing a novel about a trader on Puka Puka with the name of "Javan Moonlight."

But 1938 was a bad year. The mother of the four children became so ill with tuberculosis that Ropati could not do his daily stint at the typewriter. When in August a British warship, *H.M.S. Leith*, called at Puka Puka, he obtained permission to leave on her with his wife and his son Jakey. At Apia, Western Samoa, the wife was given a strenuous treatment with a new system called pneumothorax, but after four months the disease was found to be fatal. The doctors forbade Frisbie from taking his wife back to her home island to die, but he threatened to burn down the hospital if his wishes were not granted. Back in a thatched new house at Ngake, Puka Puka, the young wife died in Ropati's arms. It was January 14, 1939, and he was a widower with four small children to be reared in the South Seas.

It was expected that Frisbie would marry again, since the people of the atoll believed that no man could possibly bring up four little children. But stubborn Ropati could not agree. As he wrote to James Norman Hall, his main correspondent in his later years, "I failed to see why a man cannot bring up children as well as a woman can, and now, after seven months' experience, I know that he can. All this 'only a mother knows' is rubbish. A man is quite as capable as a woman, though usually he is too lazy to take on the job. Often he is better equipped. He is not apt to spoil his children by sloppy sentiment. He makes them self-reliant." That he made his atoll offspring fully reliant is evidenced again and again in the writings of his eldest daughter, Whiskey Johnny. Along with Hall's essay, "Frisbie of Danger Island" in his volume *The Forgotten One* (1952), Johnny's two books are the chief sources for the story of Robert Dean Frisbie's declining years. Her titles are *Miss Ulysses from Puka-Puka* (1948), written with much help from her father when she was only fifteen years old, and *The Frisbies of the South Seas* (1959).

After the death of his beloved wife Nga, who appears in his various writings under the name of "Desire," Ropati's three main goals were the rearing of his "four cowboys"; the hope that he could build his "little boat" and travel around the Pacific with his family as a South Sea trader; and his compulsion to write great literature. Grimly, but with feverish energy, he would go back to his battered typewriter until despair would make him quit, heartsick. As he wrote to Hall from his Puka Puka hideaway on Matauea Point: "If I could only kill this cursed desire to write I could be happy. How can you expect a man who writes in English and thinks in Puka Pukan to be able to know what kind of work he is doing?" But he was greatly encouraged when a letter of acceptance from the editor of the *Atlantic Monthly* wrote: "It is a delicious mixture of present and past . . . . There are months when the *Atlantic* cries out for good graphic humor such as this." Rare compliments of this sort were Frisbie's "emergency rations."

The author must have been elated when his first published novel, *Mr. Moonlight's Island,* appeared in 1939. The setting is Puka Puka, and the heroines are three comely, uninhibited Polynesian maidens—Miss

Red-Jones, Miss Tern, and Miss Tears (the last of these was modeled on Frisbie's wife). Reviewers were friendly, but some readers might consider this book a novelized version of *The Book of Puka-Puka*, lacking the earlier gusto. Yet Ropati still had an inked ribbon in his typewriter and continued to hope for a masterpiece.

At the height of one of Frisbie's periods of restless yearning for travel, he decided to take his four cowboys on a lengthy cruise among the islands of the South Pacific. It was just a few days after Christmas, 1941, but nobody on Puka Puka had heard that the United States had been plunged into World War II by the bombing of the fleet at Pearl Harbor. When on a stormy afternoon the ketch *Taipan* arrived off the atoll to take away the five Frisbies on their projected odyssey, Yato Beach was thronged with friends and relatives, and the scene resounded with tragic wails. Such a farewell, to these islanders, was more than a little death, for the chance that a family with deep roots in this tiny spot in the endless ocean would return there was almost zero.

The voyagers got as far as an atoll some two hundred and fifty miles to the southeast, uninhabited Suwarrow, on which Ropati and Nga had stayed for three months some years earlier. It had been discovered by the crew of the Russian-American armed ship *Suvarov* in 1814 and named for the vessel, but it remained a desolate swampy spot frequented only by occasional divers for pearl shell. To almost every human being on earth, this collection of some twenty-five tiny islets would indeed be a desert spot to shun, but Ropati and his four part-Polynesian children found it a paradise that could be an enduring home.

Life on Suwarrow was too idyllic to encourage the production of literature, and Frisbie's solitude was disturbed when "his" island was invaded by three surveyors from New Zealand and three Manihiki native helpers. Not long after, two wandering yachtsmen moored their vessel at Anchorage Island. And only a few days later, Suwarrow Atoll was virtually destroyed by one of the most terrible hurricanes ever to hit that part of the Pacific.

Thirteen human beings dwelt on Anchorage on February 19, 1942, including three little girls and a little boy, but despite that unlucky number, all of them survived. Seas as high as fifteen feet beat for days over the highest dunes inland, and the yacht *Vagus* vanished forever in the raging seas. As Ropati wrote to Hall: "Most of the land the three white men were surveying when we came here is now under the sea or in the bottom of the lagoon."

The most authentic account of the great Suwarrow hurricane that reduced the atoll to a few sand-banks is to be found in Frisbie's 1944 volume, *The Island of Desire.* This book actually deals with two islands—Puka Puka and Suwarrow. The first half recounts in nostalgic prose the life of the trader on Puka Puka and his courting of "Desire." The second part, narrating the adventures of his four children after the death of their mother, culminates with the hurricane episode. As one newspaper reviewer remarked about the author: "His story, completely out of this warring world, provides some of the best reading for pure enjoyment that has turned up for many months, and supplies as well a description of a hurricane that couldn't be bettered."

After several weeks, the survivors sailed north on Andy Thomson's *Tiare Taporo* to Manihiki, which Ropati had visited with his two friends in 1923. Even before the schooner was moored off the beach of this atoll, which claimed to hold the most beautiful sirens in all Polynesia, Ropati sighted the girl that would become his second wife. Esetera was about twenty years old, mature and graceful, a perfect hedonist who won the approval of the "four cowboys" to whom she would be a new mother.

So long as the family lived the atoll life on Manihiki,

all went like a balmy dream. However, when Frisbie took his family to Rarotonga and began desperate attempts to do his bit in World War II by joining the United States Intelligence Service, Esetera changed completely. The attractions of film theaters and night clubs proved demoralizing and she had to be sent back to Manihiki, leaving the four children to rear themselves once more, with the help of a distracted father. They went to school for the first time in their lives, struggled with the pitfalls of learning the English tongue, and were organized as a "slave-labor gang," with each child performing his listed duties.

Even distant Rarotonga—an isolated high island that had been re-discovered by Fletcher Christian and his *Bounty* mutineers in 1978 in their search for a hideaway—was too civilized for Robert Dean Frisbie. The call of Puka Puka could not be resisted. After a Christmas party for the children, he embarked with them on the *Tiare Taporo*, working his passage by serving as chief engineer. On the trip they paused at Manihiki, and found the divorced second mother, Esetera, sitting on the porch of her house, singing to "a beautiful, well-oiled brown baby." She had married a husky Manihikan and was once more a happy island girl.

When the schooner docked at Tongareva, where Ropati's old half-Maori friend Philip Woonton lived at Omoka, the Frisbies decided that Puka Puka could wait a while, and settled on the island first visited in 1777 by Captain Stavers of H.M.S. *Lady Penrhyn.*

One day the United States Navy at Pago Pago was called to evacuate an American veteran of World War I who was believed to be dying at Tongareva. Aboard the plane was Lieutenant James A. Michener, who had heard many stories about Frisbie, the "atoll man" who had "infuriated governments and encouraged native rebellion." He found on the island a totally emaciated victim of T.B.: "with his deep eyes and protruding lower jaw he looked like the dying Robert Louis Stevenson." During the flight back, the Macmillan editor and the Pacific author spent two hours conversing, and planned to write a book together one day. Ropati was taken ashore carrying at least twenty superb yellow pearls as presents for the doctors at the Pago Pago hospital.

To the surprise of everyone, Frisbie's hemorrhages were halted and he was discharged by those doctors. The four children joined him later, after their first, thrilling airplane ride. They found that their amazing father was now a teacher and acting principal of the local high school for boys. One day Michener found him lying under a pandanus tree, "drinking bush beer while his daughter Johnny taught his classes." The girl could keep better discipline, Ropati explained, than he could himself. Each night he instructed her in the next day's lesson and she would stand barefooted in a sarong, hammering English into the heads of Samoan youths in an open *fale* on a hillside.

"If she can do that," Michener said impulsively, "she can write a book. And if she does, I'll get it published." He was as good as his word.

In Samoa, Frisbie finished another novel. *Amaru: a Romance of the South Seas* was published during the final year of World War II. It details the adventures of a young American in search of a fortune in pearls on a distant islet. The reviewer for the *New York Times* was more generous than most when he wrote: "The reader could hardly find a more pleasant escape than the pages of *Amaru* provide. Any resemblance between the Pacific islands in this book and those which are at present subject to examination and attack by our armed forces is strictly coincidental."

In Pago Pago, Ropati was getting to know too many Navy men who liked to take him to the local bars, and the family went to live on a ranch in Western Samoa. But the children feared that their father was working too hard, pounding out the sentences that were, in his opinion, to make his new novel his greatest. His right leg swelled often, and the fever caused him to lie so motionless that Johnny feared he might have died. Then he would awake in the middle of the night and make frenzied revisions in the pages that Johnny would have to type in the morning. When the manuscript was finally received in New York, the editor was to write: "It is necessary to take out about ten thousand words in order to get it down to 125,000 words. That seems to be our limit these days for a three-dollar novel."

After a cruise to Tahiti to show his cowboys around that lovely island and to hold a happy reunion with his old friend and correspondent James Norman Hall, Frisbie was shocked to find that Hall was in California to attend the wedding of his daughter Nancy. After he spent two weeks in hospital, Ropati and the children boarded the *Tiare Taporo* and returned to Rarotonga. There, back among his beloved Polynesians, at his battered typewriter Ropati completed his biggest and last novel. It was not a *Moby Dick*.

Dawn Sails North was published early in 1949. It is an involved account of the voyaging of Sam Strickland, who seeks to confirm his legacy of part of an equatorial island. As the *Herald-Tribune* reviewer noted: "The author is at his best in his thrilling narrative of the voyage, and realism is strong enough to make one wonder why newspapers have not carried headlines of the island doings. Fascinating charts, island maps, and even house plans add to this story's interest." But Robert Dean Frisbie had failed to live long enough to enjoy such generous remarks, and the general verdict might have been that only glimpses of the author's earlier genius could be found in this final volume. That opinion is shared by most Frisbie-lovers today, who ransack the second-hand bookstores in search of every thing that Ropati ever wrote. The South Sea trader, they agree, achieved the top of his form when he typed out his first work, the classic *Book of Puka-Puka*.

Robert Dean Frisbie had died of tetanus on Rarotonga on November 18, 1948, in his early fifties. According to the second chapter of Michener's book *Return to Paradise*, Ropati had "used once too often a rusty hypodermic needle." He was a hobbling skeleton, penniless and in debt. He never returned to Puka Puka and his wife's grave, and he never finished building his one-man trading boat.

It was Michener who wrote Frisbie's obituary for *Publisher's Weekly*, asking for donations to help the five orphan survivors (Charles and Jakie would go to New Zealand to learn to be jockeys). And it was Jim Michener who wrote Ropati's epitaph in his chapter on "atoll men": "I liked Frisbie. I respected his basic honesty. If ever I knew a man who destroyed himself through the search for beauty, Frisbie was that man. I can respect the uncompromising artist, and I never once met Frisbie but what I pitied him and liked him, too. There were other atoll men of whom I could not say as much."

A. GROVE DAY
University of Hawaii

Introduction

I AM a South Sea trader on the atoll of Puka-Puka, or Danger Island, as it is marked on the hydrographic charts. If you search diligently you should find a dot smaller than a fly-speck on a line whose ends touch Lima, Peru, and the northeast point of Australia. Perhaps the dot doesn't appear to the naked eye. In that case, if you are still interested, intersect the first line with a second running from San Francisco to the northwest cape of New Zealand, and a third traversing the Pacific from Shanghai to the Horn. Where the three lines cross you will either find Danger Island or you won't, depending on whether the hydrographer thought it worth while to mark such an insignificant crumb of land. In any case you will agree that the spot is a sufficiently lonely one.

Danger Island comprises a reef six or seven miles in circumference, three small islets threaded on this reef, and a lagoon so clear that one can see the submerged coral mountain ranges ten fathoms below. The islets are little more than banks of sand and bleached coral where coconut-palms, pandanus, and a few grotesque, gale-twisted trees and shrubs break momentarily the steady sweep of the trade-wind. The bizarre stunted trees on the windward beaches defy both the poverty of the soil and the depredations of the Puka-Pukans, who lop off branches to make drums and popguns, coffins for dead babies, and poles on which to hang spirit charms.

But when a hurricane comes, hundreds of trees are blown down and the little Puka-Pukan houses are carried away like so many card-castles. Away goes everything then—drums, popguns, coffins, spirit charms, and sometimes a man or two, whirled with his household gods to Maroroyi, the legendary land of the departed. At such times the Puka-Pukans scramble up the stoutest coconut-palms, hack off the fronds that have not already been blown away, and roost among the stumps until the gale blows over and the seas subside.

But for years on end Puka-Puka is untroubled by great storms. Then the weeks and months slip serenely by, their monotony broken only by the yearly, or semi-yearly, arrival of Captain Viggo's trading schooner.

I hunted long for this sanctuary. Now that I have found it, I have no intention, and certainly no desire, ever to leave it again.

R. D. F.

Puka-Puka, August, 1929.

TABLE
OF
CONTENTS

Contents

I

To the Last Port of Call

Tupu toku manako m'i Tawiti:
"Ke wano 'u ki nga wenua,
Ya yoro pe te wui papaa,
Uru u i te wenua mamao."

The thought came to me in Tahiti:
"I shall sail away like the white man,
I shall paddle to some distant country,
I shall hunt in some amorous land."

—*From* "Mako Manuwiri" (*a wanderer's chant*).

To the Last Port of Call

ONE by one remote islands were left astern, trackless stretches of ocean crossed, storms weathered, and long glassy calms wallowed through. The monotonous sea days wore slowly away and still the schooner moved farther and farther into a lonely sea, visiting islands even more remote from the populous haunts of men. I realized at last that the end of my journey was at hand.

Since childhood I have always liked to reach the ends of things, finding a curious fascination in walking to the farthest point of a promontory, in climbing to the top of a mountain, or exploring the headwaters of a river; but I confess that I have never yet found the elusive apple of gold I have always hoped to find at the end of each journey. Nevertheless, I have wandered on, not over the well-traveled sea-tracks dear to the hearts of tourists, but to strange and lonely places dear to my own heart, hidden in the farthermost seas. Such a place, I knew, was the atoll

Puka-Puka (or Danger Island, as it is commonly called), and I looked forward eagerly to my arrival there.

I had left Rarotonga as a representative of the Line Islands Trading Company, with a commission to take stock in Table Winning's store on Penrhyn Island, to transact a pearl deal on Manihiki, and to go on to Puka-Puka, where I was to open and manage a store of my own.

We were three whites aboard the *Tiaré*—Captain Viggo, Prendergast the supercargo, and myself. The captain, "Papa Viggo," as he is called among the islands, is a fair-haired man, rather under average height, and with a tendency toward rotundity. He is one of those lovable, convivial souls who bring good cheer by their mere presence; but when his path is crossed, or when he is played a shabby trick, a cold glint comes into his eyes and one realizes that this quiet, easy-going Dane has another side to his character, compounded of all the sternness of his viking forefathers. Viggo is the life of the Line Islands Trading Company, versatile, shrewd, generous, and a past-master in the art of mixing rum punches.

Prendergast the supercargo, now a trader on one of the northern islands, is a cockney of forty, who spins long yarns about his pugilistic successes and his sanguinary sharp-shooting record in the war. He has a whole arsenal of guns and revolvers in the supercargo's cabin and loves to fondle, polish, and oil them, but I have never seen him shoot at anything except bottles thrown overboard or a dry piece of coral on a reef. He is much too kind-hearted even to slaughter edible sea-birds, and reserves all his ferocity for his tales of killing Germans or of how with his puissant fists he broke the head of some island champion. He himself believes the long, absurd stories with which he beguiles his friends when the punch is flowing freely. Although not particularly handsome, he is a great favorite with the island girls, much to the depletion of his purse, for he is as generous as he is boastful, and all the girls know this.

That was my first trip north with Viggo, but I had visited most of the islands before. By "north" I mean north of Rarotonga, for we never sail above the equator. Island after island was left astern: Man-

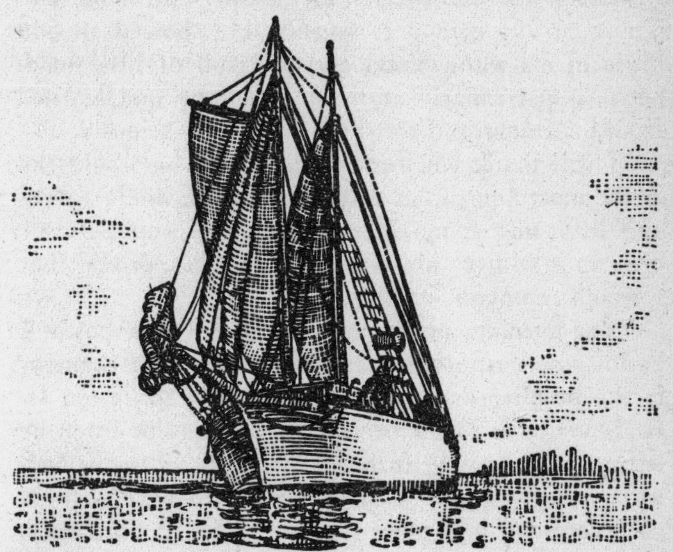

gaia, Mauke, Mitiaro, Atiu, Aitutaki, and the farther we pushed on, the more clearly I realized that a barrier was falling between me and the outside world as impenetrable as the jungle curtain which fell behind Mungo Park when he sought the outlet to the Niger.

A month went by and we sighted our first atoll, Palmerston Island, a place inhabited by the descendants, in the second, third, and fourth generation, of William Marsters, a sea captain who had retired to Palmerston with three wives and had followed the biblical counsel to increase and multiply.

I went ashore at Palmerston, weighed in thirty tons of copra, and met the son of the original William Marsters. He bears his father's Christian name and is now an old man past seventy. He showed an odd pride in his white blood and was full of little mannerisms, particularly at table, which he had learned from his father and to which he held tenaciously.

"I will thank you for the duff, sir," he would say in the most punctilious way, and when I would forget and leave my spoon in my teacup he would fix his eyes on it with an air of such severe disapproval that I would remove it at once.

That evening, under the inspiration of a bottle I had brought ashore, he sang innumerable sea chanteys in the peculiar degenerate English of Palmerston Island. When at last I became too drowsy to listen he led me to my room, furnished with an enormous bed, wide enough for at least six people to have slept in with comfort, and piled high with kapok mattresses.

Then, having given me a complete and detailed history of this bed for a period of at least sixty years, he retired with a reeling step to finish the bottle alone.

Under an ancient tamanu-tree behind the house some girls were singing. Palmerston Island girls are unusually pretty. I decided that I was not sleepy after all and slipped quietly out under the stars.

II

Our next stop was Penrhyn Island, or Tongareva, as the natives call it.

"Look out for Table Winning, 'e's no blinkin' good," Prendergast warned me as we were watching the low line of Penrhyn rise above the horizon. He then went on with a long-winded story about a fight he'd had with Winning and what a whale of a licking he, Prendergast, had given him, ending up with his usual appeal for corroboration to the captain: "Ain't that so, Viggo?" And Viggo, as usual, said "No, not a word of it," whereupon Prendergast looked surprised and hurt for a moment—but only for a moment. He was never abashed for long and consoled himself on this occasion by up-ending the last of a bottle of rum he had been carefully saving all the voyage for his old friend Winning.

Two hours later, when the *Tiaré* came alongside the landing-place at Penrhyn, the supercargo spun poor Winning a long yarn about the missing bottle, and he told it so convincingly that I almost believed it myself. But Winning was not fooled. He knew

Prendergast of old and that he could no more be trusted to carry a bottle of liquor to a friend than he could be trusted not to drop his h's.

After finishing my stock-taking I loafed rather dejectedly about Winning's trading-station until we were ready to sail for Manihiki. I was wondering all this while what the future might have in store for me at Puka-Puka. Would I find there the realization of my dreams of an island solitude? Already I had wandered far and wide over the Pacific, and the conviction grew upon me that the real glamour of the South Seas had been off for a hundred years. Men newly arrived among the islands often refuse to accept the fact that civilization, so called, has long since destroyed their charm. I myself had been among those who try to delude themselves, who try to distort the reality into some semblance of the dream; but thus far, wherever I had gone, the truth eventually forced itself upon me. Tahiti, for example, the most romantically beautiful island in all the South Seas, had become nothing more than a cheap tourist resort, and I found conditions much the same on other islands. But at Puka-Puka—there surely I could live my life in accordance with my own ideas of what constitutes living; there I could be as indolent as I pleased, as lonely as I pleased, never disturbed by the hateful thought that it is my duty to become a useful cog in the clockwork of "Progress."

Meanwhile, here we were still at Penrhyn, and I had Winning's papers to look through. Some of them were of a rather curious nature. Among other things,

I found a receipt from the Penrhyn Island administrator which read as follows:

Penrhyn Island Administration
To Table Winning:

Received the sum of nineteen shillings and six pence (19/6) for one marriage and one divorce.

Dated this 18th day of December, 19—

W——, Resident Agent.

Winning was getting on in years and had had many matrimonial adventures during the course of his life as a trader, but evidently he had not yet given up the hope of finding the ideal island mate he was forever talking about.

Another paper was an invoice of goods from a Rarotongan firm:

Cook Islands Trading Company

To Table Winning, Dr.

1	cane chair	2	5	0
1	tin cigarettes		4	0
1	case Crown ale	4	0	0
1	volume poems		7	6
	Total	6	16	6

This was a bill for Winning's personal supplies for a period of six months. Of course, he got his tinned meats, rice, flour, tobacco, etc., from his own store, and the island itself furnished fish, coconuts, birds and birds' eggs, and *puraka* (atoll taro). Winning had learned the secret of a simple life. With such food as this he was more than content, and his personal effects were so few that if ever he were to leave the island, all of them excepting the cane chair and one or two other articles of furniture could easily be packed in a single small wooden chest. And yet he was considered a rich man among the islands. He received a good salary and had earned fat sums in addition as the result of his speculations in pearls.

He has an interesting library, not a great many volumes, but all of them books worth owning. Among others I remember "The Life of Benvenuto Cellini," a couple of volumes of Louis Becke's tales, Taine's "English Literature," "Gil Blas," Blavatsky's "Caves and Jungles of Hindustan," "Lavengro," a set of "Cook's Voyages," and jammed upside down between a copy of Mungo Park's "Journal" and a thumbed and dog-eared "Shaving of Shagpat" was a faded, scarlet-backed volume with the title: "Flagellation and the Flagellants: A History of the Rod," by the Rev. William M. Cooper, B.A. I knew Table Winning well enough to be sure that that volume had strayed into his library by chance and was not one of his own choosing, and, indeed, on the fly-leaf was the name of a German trader in Samoa, a man of evil reputation. Winning's wholesome, walruslike face wrinkled with horror when he saw me glancing through the book.

"Ropati!" he said earnestly, "I don't think I'd read that if I were you."

III

A few days later we went on to Manihiki, and pretty Manihiki girls dressed for the occasion in their bright print gowns came aboard in swarms, bringing us hats of native manufacture for presents, and fans dyed all the colors of a tropical sunset. And the men came with bunches of drinking coconuts; and immediately, of course, there was dancing on the decks of the little *Tiaré*. Every one but Captain Viggo forgot that there was copra ashore to be weighed, and at last he was reluctantly compelled to suggest that the merrymaking be postponed until later. And so it was; but not long after sundown we heard the booming of great sharkskin drums and, with our work done, we hurried in the direction of the music.

We all danced that night: Viggo, Prendergast, myself—even the somber-faced but golden-hearted resident agent could not withstand the weird heathen rhythms thundered out by the drums. There were several of these drums, each with its name painted in glaring red letters around its ten-foot circumference. One was called Little Blind Queen of the Flower Garden (*Ariki-Vaine Matopo no te Kainga Tiaré*). Another bore the yet more appealing legend, Alas! My Love, the Morning Breaks! (*Aué! Toku Akaperepere, kua Popongi!*) Everybody dances at Manihiki, from the babies just old enough to walk to the great-grandmothers and great-grandfathers; and how they put us stiff-jointed whites to shame! We spent three days at the island, during which time I stayed ashore with our trader, an exceptionally fine half-caste with a physique like that of some old Roman gladiator and a mind as ingenuous as a child's. He gave me a priceless recipe for raisin wine which I will whisper to the thirsty reader in due time.

IV

Three months had passed since we left Rarotonga, months of light winds and lingering calms when for days together we lay motionless, lazily rocked on the backs of the long Pacific rollers. A fresh breeze would make up at times, only to die quickly away as though the spirit presiding in that empty sea were reluctant to carry us to our last and loneliest port of call.

"Only twenty-five miles since yesterday," the captain would say. "Ropati, I'm afraid you'll be an old man before we reach Puka-Puka."

We called at Rakahanga, Suvarrow, Nassau, this last a tiny green spot inhabited by not more than a dozen families. We stood by for an hour or two while the men came out in their canoes to gaze blankly at us.

Presently Viggo hailed them, asking if there was anything they wanted.

One man started as though roused from sleep, and after a long silence he said, "I'd like some fish-hooks, about ten, I think."

"Well, I'll be blowed! Is that all?" Prendergast yelled. Their canoes were close by, but it seemed necessary to shout to rouse them from their deep midday trances.

"I don't know. I think so," came the reply.

Viggo laughed good-naturedly. "Give him his fish-hooks and let's get under way," he said. Prendergast tossed him a small box of hooks and again we crept on toward Danger Island.

But the next morning Nassau was still only a few miles astern.

About noon four canoes loaded with copra came alongside, for the Nassau people had suddenly wakened to the fact that a ship had come from that vague world beyond the horizon, bringing ribbons, stick candy, and all kinds of desirable things. They clambered aboard, their eagerness in strange contrast to their apathy of the day before, crowded into the trade-room, and soon they were loaded down with useless trifles. One old man, wiser than the rest, bought a hank of fish-line, and a very pretty girl with sparkling black eyes had no trouble at all in wheedling me out of a used typewriter-ribbon. She immediately bound up her hair with this, tying it in fantastic knots and streamers, smiling and giggling as she did so, while I held Prendergast's mirror before her, half afraid that she would leave off when she realized what a purple mess the ribbon was making of her pretty face. But this only pleased her the more. She rubbed the loose ends of the ribbon over her cheeks and nose and then ran on deck whooping like a schoolboy, or rather like the pretty little savage she was. I looked regretfully into the mirror, with the vague hope that such a bewitching image could never be lost, but only my own dumb features met my gaze.

For yet another day Nassau was in sight; then a light wind carried us as far as Tema Reef. This is a circular piece of coral more than a half a mile across, a submarine mountain with precipitous sides rising miles above the unlit depths of the surrounding ocean floor to within a few feet of the surface. The seas break on all sides of it with deafening concussion and rush foaming to the center of the reef, where they meet with terrific impact to rise, geyserlike, a hundred feet above the boiling shallows.

At dusk we were close by the reef. Hundreds of sharks circled about the schooner, gobbling the albacore that took our trolling-spoons long before we could haul them half-way to the ship. Viggo pointed out the rusty iron stem of a vessel embedded in the living coral. It rose above the reef with an air of reckless, hopeless valor, and the waves broke on its sides as they had done decades ago when she was a living thing, loved by some deep-sea skipper whose bones now lie in the fathomless depths below. It made a forlorn and desolate picture in the gathering gloom. I was glad when we had left it well astern.

Yet another day we wallowed lazily over the long undulations, but at sunset Viggo led me to the cabin-top, where he pointed out a tenuous black line breaking for a brief space the smooth circle of the horizon. Clouds hung over it, and from the farther side a golden sunset light streamed down, throwing the tiny crumb of land into intensely black relief. The schooner lumbered down the slope of the swell, and the island vanished.

"There's your Puka-Puka," said Viggo, "and my last port of call, thank God!"

A sharp puff of wind rattled the stops against the mainsail, and from the cabin below I heard the drawling notes of Prendergast's accordion.

When I came on deck the following morning the schooner was resting easily in the lee of Puka-Puka. A fresh trade-wind ruffled the surface of the lagoon, for now that we were at our journey's end the long calm, too, was at an end, and the breeze seemed to be urging us to leave this lonely place, to return to the world we had come from.

To the south was the reef I have already spoken of, with a haze of sunlight-filtered mist hanging over the foaming breakers. A shorter tongue of reef lay to the north and the lagoon was to the east, its clear water mottled by splotches of vivid coloring. I saw three islets, one at each corner of a triangular reef which completely encircled the lagoon.

Near-by some men were fishing from canoes. Now and then they would glance indifferently at us, in strange contrast to the natives of some of the islands, who, the moment the schooner was sighted, would paddle eagerly out to meet her and clamber aboard, shouting and gesticulating, eager to buy things—to steal them too—and to get the news from other islands.

"Now there's Puka-Puka for you," said Viggo, pointing toward the canoes. There was a slight note of resentment in his tone. "The arrival of my schooner doesn't mean as much to these people as their Wednesday night *himené*. Look at the islet there, the horseshoe-shaped one where the settlements are: half a dozen children on the beach and no one else. Very likely their fathers and mothers don't even know that we've come. The island is as dead asleep as it was before the three-fingered god Maui fished it out of the sea. Everything is asleep here; I never made the island except in a series of calms, and the wind singing through the palms seems to make you drowsier at Puka-Puka than it does at other islands. The people see no reason at all for getting up in the morning, and most of 'em don't: they sleep all day, but at night they wake up, and you'll see them fishing by torchlight off the reef—eating, dancing, love-making on shore. Trading skippers—the few that know Puka-Puka—hate the island because they can't get people to work loading their ships; but I've always liked the place.

After all, why should they work, for me or for any one else? There's not a single article in my trade-room that they really need. When they sell me copra and buy my goods they are no more than accommodating me. They know it, too—that's the worst of it."

"There's six women to every man," Prendergast broke in. "Ain't that so, Viggo?"

"No," Viggo replied, as usual. Then he laid his hand on my arm in a fatherly manner. "Ropati, you've seemed out of spirits most of this trip north, though I must say you brightened up a bit at Manihiki and Nassau. Now tell me, honestly: do you really want to stop at this out-of-the-way place? You won't see another white man till I come back again, six or eight months from now. You can't speak the language, and the natives will treat you about as friendly as those fishermen are treating us. You'll be very lonesome, and you know white men often go insane under such conditions as you'll find here. I'll leave you, if you're sure you want to stay; but if you've changed your mind, speak out now. I'll take you back with me and there'll be no harm done."

That's the way it was with Viggo: always fatherly, kind-hearted, and considerate of others even to the prejudice of his own interests. I glanced at the nearest islet dozing in the morning sunlight, with only two or three languid columns of smoke rising above the trees to tell of the life ashore. I thought of my long search in the Pacific for an island where I would be a law to myself and beyond reach of even the faintest echo from the noisy clamor of the civilized world. I thought of my little library of five or six hundred books boxed up in the hold, and of my half dozen kegs of fine old liquor smuggled from Tahiti. Then I visualized myself in a cool thatched hut, my brow fanned by the trade-wind, and a charming Puka-Puka girl ready to fill my pipe and to bring me tall rum punches. Contentment's motherly hand already seemed to rest on me soothingly. Here no officious relatives or friends would cry: "Young man, you are wasting your life! Here you are, nearing thirty, with nothing accomplished, with no plans for the future, with no bank account! You must reform! It is your duty to help keep the wheels of Industry moving! Be efficient! Abstain from alcohol and tobacco! Join the church! Study Pelmanism!"

I squeezed Viggo's arm. "No, I want to stay," I said. "Can I take my things ashore now? I'll come out in the morning to say good-by."

Viggo turned to Prendergast. "You'd better go with him," he said, "and try and arrange with Kare to rent his big coral-lime house for a store. Then you can check over the trade goods I send ashore. Ropati will have enough to do to-day getting settled."

II

Sea Foam the Christian and William the Heathen

Ka noo 'u i te aroaro no te Atua;
Kaakaa i toku kak'u lelei.
Ono-ono 'u i te auwi i te Po
Ke tunu i te mango ma te kiore,
Ke tunu i te tutae-auri!

I sit at the feet of God;
Bright are my beautiful clothes.
I gaze into the fires of Hell,
Where sharks, rats, and heathens
Are writhing in the flames.

—*From* "Mako Pure" (*a Puka-Puka religious chant*).

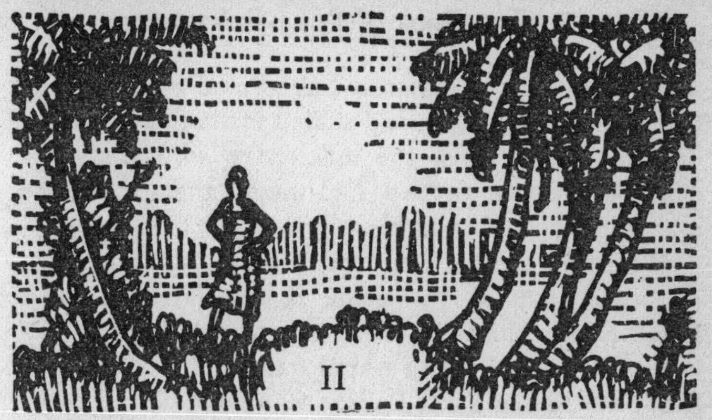

Sea Foam the Christian and William the Heathen

AFTER crossing the reef we pulled the boat over a long stretch of shallow water, rowed across a bay formed within the bight of the main islet, and ran her stem upon a white coral beach. A few sleek-skinned children came running, open-mouthed, stopped abruptly a few yards away, and stood motionless.

An old woman with a grass skirt tied over a ragged gown of cheap print, sat in front of a hut to our left. She gesticulated in a frenzied, incoherent manner, smiling and nodding her head at us. Prendergast greeted her in Rarotongan, calling her "Mama" (Metua-vainé). At this she gesticulated more frantically than ever, cackling like an old witch, but I noticed that her teeth were beautifully white.

"It's old Mama," Prendergast explained; "she's William's wife, and a fine old lady she is, too!"

We shook hands with her. The hand-shaking ceremony is still fairly recent at Puka-Puka. Formerly the islanders rubbed noses and sniffed in true native style, but the Rev. Johns, the missionary who visits the island every year or two, had taught them the white man's manner of greeting.

While we were talking with Mama, Kare Moana, or Sea Foam, as the name is translated—I shall avoid native names in these memoirs when they can be rendered in English—appeared on the scene. He is one of the few Puka-Pukans who have visited other islands, and the only one, I think, who has ever seen foreign countries. He had passed through New Zealand and Australia on his way to Papua, where, in fever-stricken coastal lands, he did missionary work for which the white missionaries got all the credit. He was dressed in new denim trousers, a "boiled shirt," with a celluloid collar, and a funny little black necktie fastened askew. He wore a bandmaster cap decorated with gold braid. It was much too small for him and sat on the top of his round head in a supercilious manner, as though conscious of the fact that it was the only bandmaster cap on the island.

Sea Foam greeted us in Rarotongan, which he spoke fluently, although every few sentences he would change abruptly into old biblical Tahitian; and when he spoke of his house he always called it "my *la maison.*" This was the single French expression he had picked up at Tahiti. In the curious native fashion he asked me whether I were alive? hungry? thirsty? Did I wish to sleep? How many brothers did I have? How many sisters? How old were they? What was the color of their eyes? their hair? etc., etc. When I had replied to his various questions he assured me that I was a fine fellow, by far the best white man who had ever landed at Puka-Puka. All this was in the Tahitian dialect. Then, in Rarotongan, he said that he would feed me as long as I stayed on the island. This was a thing any native would say, but Sea Foam to a large extent actually carried out his promise.

Turning, he shouted in an unfamiliar guttural tongue, and immediately a small boy ran out of a hut, "walked" up a coconut-palm like a monkey on a stick, and threw down some green drinking-nuts. He slid down, grabbed the nuts, husked them with his teeth, and handed them to Prendergast and me. Then he vanished, doubtless to sleep again. His little act was performed as quickly and beautifully as a conjurer's trick.

After our drink, Prendergast talked business with Sea Foam.

"Kare, Viggo says that since you an' 'im is old cronies, 'e's goin' to do you a favor by rentin' your coral-lime 'ouse. 'E's goin' to give you a quid a month."

Sea Foam's face displayed neither pleasure nor displeasure. "Ah, yes," he said gravely. "My fine new *la maison*. There are two stories and a floor of real boards for the upper story. It has the finest thatch roof on the island."

"Never mind about that. We know what a blinkin' fine 'ouse it is, an' 'ow it gets the ague every time the wind blows. You're satisfied, are you—a quid a month?"

"Ah, well, Viggo and I are as brothers. I should be ashamed to refuse him anything, so you can tell him I will let him have my *la maison* for two pounds a month."

"Two wot? See 'ere, Kare! Viggo said I was to arsk Ura and Rori in case you wouldn't be sensible about that old shack of yours. Two pounds! Strike me bleedin' well pink! It ain't worth ten bob!" The supercargo winked foxily at me.

Sea Foam stroked his chin thoughtfully.

"Ah, well," he said, "you'd better speak to Rori

or Ura, then. Now about our copra: we won't be able to load the schooner this week or next week either. We are having a church festival, and the Reverend Johns would never forgive me if we worked during the festival."

Prendergast pulled a long face. "Oh, have it your own way, Kare. We ain't partin' brass rags about a blitherin' quid. We'll pay you two quid for yer fine new *la maison*. Now, then, 'ow about the church festival? You ain't goin' to 'old up the ship for any jamboree like that, are you?'

"Oh, mercy, no!" said Sea Foam in his soft voice. "The Reverend Johns would never forgive me if I kept Captain Viggo waiting."

II

An hour later I passed through the central village where the trading-station was to be, and, turning into a path which led behind the great coral-and-thatch church, walked through a desolate graveyard and on to the coconut-groves and taro-beds of the interior. It had been long since I had stretched my legs, so I took advantage of Prendergast's good nature, leaving him to check over the trade goods Viggo was sending ashore.

Inland, as much as fifty acres had been excavated to a depth of ten feet, bringing the taro-beds to sea level, where the roots of the plants could flourish in swampy ground. This work must have required many years to complete, for there were no tools but coconut-shells with which to scoop out the sand. In these beds *puraka* and bananas also thrived, making one forget that Puka-Puka is an atoll.

While skirting the first taro excavation I heard a cry from the village: "Paji! Paji!" The word is sufficiently like the Rarotongan one for ship to inform me that at last the inhabitants were waking to the fact that Viggo had come. Looking back, I saw that the sleepy little village was now astir. Fathers and mothers were stumbling out into the blazing sunlight, and funny little naked children were running back and forth in great excitement.

I wandered on, past a dozen or more taro-beds and as many desolate little graveyards isolated among the groves. The island is dotted with these burying-grounds, for the graves of the discoverers of the island and all their descendants are still intact. They are weird places, with headstones of coral slabs covered with innumerable designs. The inclosures are bare of vegetation; they gulp the hot sunlight voraciously and give it back in scorching waves of heat. Later I heard many remarkable stories about these graveyards: the entire history of the island may be read there, and the shape of each stone is distinctive, relating the story of the individual buried beneath.

Near the sea side of the islet the taro-beds give place to coconut-groves, for here the sand has been banked from twenty to thirty feet high. Trees with gale-gnarled limbs grow by the beach, sheltering the palms, and beyond is scraggly bush which gains meager sustenance from the coral gravel thrown up by the sea.

On breaking my way through the bush I closed my eyes before the glare of exposed sand and the shallow water between the reef and the shore, reflecting the full blaze of the sun like countless mirrors. The shallows were alive with cross-seas meeting in sparkling ridges of spray, falling back in dancing undulations. Miniature waves washed up on the beach, which gulped them down, leaving no backwash; and from farther out came the incessant thundering of the great Pacific combers as they rose high to crash in resounding cannonades along the reef and to spill back into the sea, exposing rust-red ridges of coral broken by pools of sea-foam.

I came to a point of the islet where, beyond the reef, seas from both north and south swing round the land to meet with tremendous impact. That morning I could enjoy watching these great seas wrecking each other, but later, after I had been washed over the reef in the midst of a gale, I could not pass this point of Teauma without a shudder.

III

"Ulekaina!" croaked a froglike voice, so close at hand that I was slightly startled. I looked about, but at first saw no one. Then, to one side, I observed a mound of coconut leaves somewhat resembling a small hayrick. A grizzled brown head protruded from the top of it, and a face furrowed all over with deep wrinkles. On the head was the brim of a European straw hat; the crown was missing; the head thus framed was shaped as nearly like a blunt-nosed bullet as a cast could have made it. Under the brim a pair of small shrewd eyes regarded me closely, and a pair of ears, anything but small, stood out almost at right angles from the head. The skin of the face was like old, well-seasoned shoe leather, pierced on the chin by about a dozen wiry hairs that served as a beard.

"Ulekaina!" the voice again croaked, and of a sudden the hayrick rose and became an enormous grass skirt which covered the old man at least a foot deep. He raised a long index-finger, described a circle in the air, and then pointed at himself. "Uiliamu" (William), he said.

I described a similar circle with my index-finger, pointed to my breast-bone and said, "Ropati."

He nodded in a knowing manner, resumed his hayrick posture, and produced a pipe from somewhere in his grass skirt. Holding it to within an inch of his right eye, he stared into the empty bowl and sighed deeply. Then he brought forth an empty tin, gazed into it in the same distressing manner, and demonstrated its emptiness by turning it upside down and shaking it vigorously. I handed him my tobacco tin, whereupon he proceeded to fill his own in the good old Scots fashion, cramming the tobacco down, making far-sighted provision for the future. Having filled his tin, he again concealed it in the grass skirt and, digging into another part of the hayrick, produced a stick of tobacco and some dried pandanus leaf. With these he rolled two cigarettes, one for me, in consideration of my generosity. We smoked them in silence.

After a long and, to me, rather embarrassing interval, he said, in polished whaler English: "Where ta hell you from?"

"What?" I said. I was rather bowled over by this sudden question.

"Goddam! You no spik English? What ta hell! You Daggo? You Chow? I spik too much English. Whas a matter you?"

"I'm an American," I said. "I've come here to open a trading-station. Where did you learn English?"

"Me? What the devil! We whaler-man! Me no Puka-Puka Kanaka! Whaler-man! *Tutae-auri!*"

"Tutae-auri" means "heathen," and William went

on to assure me that he had nothing to do with Christians. This interested me, for very few of the natives on these lonely islands have the courage to flout the missionaries. Although few or none of them have more than a vague notion of what Christianity is about, nevertheless they are great church-goers. I have not met more than three who, like old William, were avowedly and boastfully heathen.

We sat for a long time on Teauma Point, yarning about all sorts of things. Once he left me for a moment to shin up a coconut-palm for drinking-nuts, as agilely as though he had temporarily shouldered off half a century. We talked until noon, when he accompanied me to the village, going before me with an air of possessorship, for he told me that he meant to adopt me as his son, exhibiting me to all the Christians as the white man whose Godlessness was equal to his own.

III

The Fine Art of Trading

Ye nga kumi!
Puke nga kie!
Rave i toku ri kura mero!
Akaperu kia ma toku tu kupu e ropa;
Wakariri i yu ra te vao;
Mana porokume nga o te motu!

Cut the cloth!
Many bolts of cloth!
Buy many yards of red ribbon!
I shall wind it about my youthful body;
I shall be stared at in the inland groves;
Oh! I shall be a power in the islands!

—*From* "Mako oko-oko i te paji" (*customer's chant when making purchases from a passing ship*).

The Fine Art of Trading

SEA FOAM'S *la maison* is a two-story building with thick walls made from blocks of chipped coral. There are two large rooms below for the store and two above for living quarters, opening to verandas both front and back. The front veranda overlooks the road and the central village, with the school-house directly opposite and the church a little to the right. The back veranda faces the lagoon and is only a few feet from the water's edge, so that when I sit there, cooled by the trade-wind, I can easily imagine that I am living on an otherwise uninhabited island. Now and then, to be sure, the silence is broken by a sleepy voice behind me, the crowing of a cock, or the monotonous drumming on coconut-shells by the village children, but these are such common, familiar sounds that often I am no more aware of them than of the wind humming through the fronds of the palms.

At other times the children's perpetual tapping on coconut-shells exasperates me. In the midst of day dreams, when extravagant desires seem to become realities and my air-castles become almost palpable to the eye, I will start suddenly, the dreams vanish into thin air, and I hear the persistent *tap, tap-tap, tap, tap-tap* stabbing through the silence with horrible distinctness. I realize that I have been thus annoyed for hours; a roar of Yankee curses thunders through the sleeping village, a high-pitched woman's voice scolds from an adjacent hut, the drumming ceases at once, and silence falls again, a silence so profound that I can hardly believe it has ever been broken.

At night I prefer sitting on my front veranda, where I can watch the village life passing below; for on this topsy-turvy little island people wake at sunset, stumble sleepily into the lagoon for a bath, and having thus refreshed themselves, start the day's activities.

On my first night at Puka-Puka I was alone. Ever-efficient Prendergast had checked over the trade goods and returned to the ship. Sea Foam brought me a mat and a mosquito-net, so I had nothing to do but unpack a few of my belongings and loll on the veranda watching the villagers waking from their long siestas.

As dusk deepened, fishermen put out in canoes, some with torches and nets for flying-fish, others with spears for the lobsters and parrot-fish of the reef. Fires flared among the houses, and groups of chattering natives strolled up and down the village street, as they have done from time immemorial. Now and then I heard a gurgle of laughter and, looking round, saw the chubby head of a naked urchin who had scrambled up one of my veranda posts to have a near view of the absurd white man. The moment he was detected he would let go, fall with a thump, and rush whooping off in the darkness.

Presently a youth of about eighteen stopped in front of my house with a number of his friends. Although it was growing dark, I could make him out dressed in a heavy British army overcoat, and his shoes squeaked gloriously. Placing his arms akimbo and generally striking a bombastic attitude he delivered a long harangue in Puka-Pukan. I did not know what he was saying; nevertheless, I can give here an almost literal translation of his speech, for these little night monologues are much the same. When a young Puka-Pukan feels that he has grown to manhood, he simply has to let off steam, and one method of doing it is to walk through the villages with his friends, stopping before every other house to make a speech. His address of welcome to me was about as follows:

"*Noo akalelei kotou kia akalongo i toku tara-tara!* Sit down prettily you people and listen to my speech! I, George, being a man of the village of Yato, son of the exceptional man whose name is Abraham, and of the woman of the village Ngake whom everybody knows to be the daughter of Ura, chief of police and sometimes deacon of the church—I, George-man, take it upon myself to inform you of the new talk that has come to my ears. I have heard that a white man has come to this island and he is called Ropati, so I lose no time in warning him to keep his pigs tied up and not to steal taro from me, my father, or my

mother, who is the daughter of the great Ura, chief of police and sometimes deacon of the church. Moreover, I warn the man, Ropati, not to steal taro, chickens, or coconuts from any of my relatives; but if he is hungry and must steal something, let him steal from my enemies.

"I, George-man, of Yato Village, a grandson of the redoubtable Ura, (etc., etc.), further warn this person, Ropati, that the young women of this island are dear to the hearts of me and my friends, and if—" but at this point George becomes altogether too outspoken and explicit to permit of translation.

He rambles on, repeating himself and taking promptings from his companions. When at last he is out of breath, his friends gather round him and all grunt a delightfully obscene chant peculiar to the island. Everybody, old and young, laughs uproariously at this and immediately forgets all about it. George and his boon companions have let off steam; they have had their fun and the little show is at an end.

II

About ten o'clock the fishing canoes returned. Then, like magic, the islet was transformed. Scores of coconut-shell fires blazed with their characteristic glaring white flame, throwing grotesque shadows on the brown thatched huts, dancing in fairylike shimmerings among the domes of coconut fronds, casting ghostly reaches of light through the adjacent graveyards, and silhouetting the forms of *pareu*-clad natives at work cleaning their fish or laying them on the live coals to broil.

I rose from my mat and walked through the village, hungrily sniffing the fragrance of fish roasting on scentless coconut-shell coals, for I had eaten nothing since morning. Now I was greeted on every side with "*Ulekaina!*" and "*moe ai koe!*" The first greeting is not translatable; the other means much the same as our "Pleasant dreams," an appropriate greeting, certainly, for such a somnolent little island. Everything is dreamlike here: the island itself is a dream come true so that romanticists who are patient enough and adventurous enough may see vindicated their faith in lonely lands beyond the farthest horizon.

On the outskirts of the Central Village, beyond the groves and the taro-beds, where lugubrious shadows played fitfully, I halted abruptly and stared at a vision so lovely that for a moment I was all but convinced it was only a vision created by my own romantic fancy.

A girl of about fourteen was sitting cross-legged, gazing into a fire of coconut husks. She was naked save for the short girdle of fern leaves about her waist, and her thick dark hair hung loosely about her shoulders. Her skin, of that velvety texture found only among Polynesian women, gave back the firelight in soft gleams. Her slim brown body was as graceful as the stem of a young coconut-palm, and light and shadow played over it caressingly. She glanced up quickly at my approach and smiled, unconscious of her nakedness. I smiled back—a foolish smile it must have been—and hurried on, conscious of the hot blood throbbing in my temples.

Upon returning, I came to Mama's house, where William hobbled out to insist on my eating with them. Old Mama seconded the invitation, gesticulating and grinning with all her might. They made an amusing pair and seemed peculiarly suited to one another. I was by no means sorry to have them for next-door neighbors.

Mama gave me a fine *malau* served on a clean banana leaf, and a piece of taro pudding. Both the fish and the pudding were wonderfully appetizing after my long ship's diet of tinned meats.

After the meal William and I talked for a long time while Mama hovered around, feeling my hair, running her long bony fingers into my pockets to examine their contents with childish delight. Everything they contained amused her, and at each discovery she would clasp her hands and make all sorts of funny little noises. She chattered ceaselessly, asking William questions to which he would reply in an offhand, disdainful manner.

Soon a crowd of natives gathered round, when William, waiting for the psychological moment, produced the tobacco he had stolen from me. He ceremoniously filled his pipe with an air that seemed to say that he never smoked any but the very finest brands of white men's tobacco, and pompously lit it with a coal from the fire. But a little later, when the others had gone, he knocked out the half-smoked tobacco with disgust and refilled the pipe with his own mule-killing twist.

III

The next morning I went out to say good-by to Viggo and Prendergast. Viggo assumed a cheery offhand manner, but I could see that he was worried, doubtful as to the advisability of leaving me here alone. Had I wished it, I am sure that he would gladly have gone to the trouble of bringing all my goods back to the ship.

But there were no misgivings in my mind as I paddled back across the reef; then I sat on the gunwales, the canoe aground in shallow water, and watched the *Tiaré* getting under way. Rounding the northern point, she swung her beam to me and I could see Viggo on the break of the poop, waving his cap; then the schooner slipped behind the coconut-palms of the leeward point. For a time the tops of her sails were visible, then only the tops of her pole-masts, until, of a sudden, she was lost wholly to view.

I was now irrevocably isolated from the world, but with a light heart I called to Benny (Peni), my newly acquired store boy. He jumped from the canoe and pulled it over the shallows to the bay.

In the course of time the store was ready. One room was equipped with rough shelves and one reserved for a storeroom. Upstairs I had my bedroom and a living-room, furnished with a table, a lamp, and an easy chair, where I stacked my books and laid out my kegs of rum. I hung an oil-painting of the brig *Sea Foam*, by Viggo, over the door and tacked a calendar by the table. These sufficed for decorative purposes.

The rest of the establishment consisted of a little cook-house where William and Mama presided in leisurely fashion, to the envy of the neighbors. They prepared all my food, which was just to my taste, for there was an abundance of sea food to satisfy my ichthyophagian appetite. Then I could buy fat young friers at a shilling each, and eggs at sixpence per dozen; so, after teaching Mama that a chicken should be decapitated before frying—a waste she greatly lamented—and that when I said the coffee was too weak it did not mean that she was to make it as thick as porridge the next morning, I got along very nicely.

When William was not fishing, chopping wood, or sleeping, he would sit in the cook-house and order Mama about with thundering curses, like some tyrannical old whaling skipper who had made the ribs of his vessel tremble with his bellowing voice. But dear old Mama was accustomed to this and did not pay the slightest attention.

I opened the store early one Monday morning. Benny and I assumed the proper attitudes behind the counter, with all our little trinkets arranged behind us in glittering rows of gilt and paint—and not a soul came to buy. Several hours passed, but toward noon a child peeped around the edge of the door holding a coconut out at arm's length. We were all attention, but unluckily, just as our first customer was about to make a purchase, his courage failed him and he rushed whooping away. Whereupon Benny and I closed the station.

No sooner were the doors closed than some of the villagers started to wake up; and while Benny and I were eating our taro tops and roast chicken, with Mama waving her arms wildly over our heads in a vain effort to keep the flies away, a little crowd of natives gathered about the store. Then they surrounded the cook-house to watch the foolish white man eating with a knife and fork. This sight always interested them.

"Ah!" said Benny, his mouth full of taro, "*if* we had only waited a few minutes longer we would have sold something." Benny's favorite word was "*if*" (*naringa*), as it is with all Puka-Pukans. Every day one continually hears such phrases as: "If I had gone fishing I would have had something to eat"; "If I had not been under the coconut-tree the nut would not have fallen on me"; "If I had put a new roof on my house"—if I had done this, that, and the other.

But Benny was not so bad in this respect as the other islanders. He had been to Rarotonga, where he had not only learned the language but had also acquired industrious habits. I gave him a little lecture on the futility of using the word "if," but I doubt whether he heard me, for he was crunching chicken bones with an appalling racket.

When we reopened the store the little space between the counter and the door was jammed with people. An old man, whom I shall call Ezekiel because his name sounds something like that, was the first customer. Elbowing his way through the crowd, he laid a pound note on the counter and in a halting voice asked for a tin of talcum-powder. He gazed timidly at the surrounding crowd, smiling when he saw a dozen heads bobbing in approbation. As I reached for the tin, there was a buzz of voices from the open doorway at the back, from the two windows, and from the crowd in front. I caught two words in the chatter: "*Paura*" (powder) and "Ezekiel." This was the old dog's day, and he was enormously puffed up with the stir he was making.

I wrapped the tin in a piece of illustrated newspaper and handed it to the old man. When I turned to count out his change he moved to the door, where he became the center of an envious group, who examined the paper while a young girl took the tin and shook the powder into her hair with screams of delight. Then every one's attention was turned to the girl; they smelled her hair, commenting in guttural tones on the fragrance of the powder, while they wrinkled up their noses and rolled out their lips like braying donkeys. At last Ezekiel retrieved his half-emptied tin and turned to leave the store. I had Benny call him back and put the change—seventeen and sixpence—in his hand.

He gazed in stupid amazement at the money, at me, at Benny, and back again at the money. Gradually a light came into his watery eyes—he understood that somehow or other it did not require all his pound to pay for a tin of talc.

His next purchase was a long strip of fiery red pongee, and the same dumfounded expression came into his eyes when I took only a part of his money. Then he bought a box of matches: he decided to play the game with this remarkable white man, to get as much as possible for his money, for it was evident that Captain Viggo's new trader didn't understand his business. Next he bought some tobacco, brass wire, fish-hooks, and a tin whistle. At last there was only sixpence left. He gazed long and wistfully at the various flashy trade goods, finally setting his choice on a red and yellow striped shirt worth—or, rather, priced—ten shillings. I tried to explain that there was not enough money left to pay for it, but he could not understand and went from the store convinced, I think, that I was cheating him.

My next customer was Ears (Taringa), the policeman of the Leeward Village, Yato. A very garrulous person, he approached the counter in a fog of verbiage. A thin, shark-toothed woman, his wife, followed in his wake, casting sharp, malicious glances at all the other possible customers. She looked enviously at Ezekiel, who was still standing in the doorway gazing at his lone sixpence; then she nudged her husband and demanded that he buy her two tins of talcum-powder, for it would be a shame to let the Ezekiel faction outdo her in powder.

Ears pretended to know how to count money. "How much for one?" he cried above the din of voices, rolling his eyes knowingly.

"Two and sixpence."

He laid down one and threepence with an air of great intelligence and then gazed abstractedly at the ceiling.

His face lengthened when I called for more, but in a moment he broke into a bellow of laughter. "A wise man, this white man," he said to the others. "I thought he might be poor at counting money, but now I see that he knows arithmetic as well as I do."

Then he scratched his head, glanced questioningly at his wife, and tucked his *pareu* more tightly about his waist. Finally he shoved ten shillings across the counter and again gazed at the ceiling. I took the correct change and shoved the rest back.

He stared at the money with a perplexed frown; then he nodded his head in a self-important manner and said: "I see that he is honest, this white man! I was testing him, I being the policeman of Leeward Village. I wanted to see if he would steal my money, but he's all right. He has given me the correct change to the last farthing!" Then with a grandiose display of erudition he fingered the coins in a mock attempt at counting, whereupon he walked out of the store very well pleased with himself. He came back later when the others had gone, to complete his purchases.

At that time, of course, I knew little of the Puka-Pukan language; it was Benny who explained later what the talk was all about. I realized that my honesty would be sorely tried on Puka-Puka, for I could charge a penny or a pound and, with the exception of a half-dozen of the ultra-learned, no one would be the wiser. I resolved on that first day never to cheat these simple-minded folk.

It was Benny, too, who told me about Ura's One Pound Trading Company, a story which fully explained Ezekiel's surprise at receiving change from his pound note.

A few years before, a gullible Papeete trading company, disastrously managed by the island-famous (and Jack London-famous) Paumotuan, Mapuhi, established a trading-station on Puka-Puka, with Ura (chief of police and sometimes deacon of the church) as trader. Although Ura was crafty, he was but little better at arithmetic than his satellite, Ears, the policeman of Leeward Village. Therefore, in order to be certain that no money was lost, Ura charged a pound sterling for each article in his store, no matter whether it was a pair of trousers or a sixpenny bottle of scent. Tobacco, matches, and fish-hooks were exceptions; these he traded for coconuts as Mapuhi had directed.

Ura weighed in copra at a pound for five bags, always going through the process of weighing for the appearance of the thing, but always paying the same price. He bought no smaller lots, claiming that his scales would not weigh less than five bags. They were steelyard scales, and, when not in service, Ura used the counterpoise iron weight for a canoe anchor. Eventually he lost the weight, but he blandly twisted a piece of wire around a lump of coral and used that quite as successfully, for five bags of copra still came to exactly one pound sterling.

Thus Mapuhi's store prospered until one day when a hurricane struck the island. The crafty chief of police managed to save the bags of store money before the seas sweeping over the island sent him up a coconut-palm. The store was completely destroyed, and when Mapuhi returned, Ura met him with a long face, deploring the act of God that had swept away the store and all the bags of money as well. But it is an open secret on the island that when other ships came, Ura spent handfuls of Chili dollars, for years wearing nothing but red silk shirts and buying bully beef by the case.

IV

A few days later, observing a number of children gathered outside the store, I opened a tin of lemon-drops, marked "lollies," after the New Zealand fashion. Benny and I ate a few and made it known that they were very good and cost only one coconut each. But the candy business was a failure until William came to the rescue, bringing a couple of coconuts he had filched from my cook-house. When he had made his purchase and was crunching his lemon-drops,

I explained that although it was quite correct for men to eat this confection, it was best suited to the tastes of the children. Despite this suggestion the old men and women started bringing me their nuts, and by noon that day every adult on the island was sucking lollies. I realized a good 500 per cent profit, which trading companies consider but a modest return from their commodities, but in so far as I know, none of the children benefited in the candy trade.

The money Viggo had paid for the island's copra was soon exhausted; then the coconut trade started in earnest. I made a price-list for Benny which still hangs in the store. It reads:

1 stick tobacco .... 8 coconuts
1 ship's biscuit............ 2 coconuts or 2 eggs
1 box matches............ 2 coconuts or 2 eggs
1 fish-hook............... 1 coconut or 1 egg
1 yard brass wire......... 1 coconut or 1 egg
1 lollie................... 1 coconut or 1 egg

From that time on, Benny looked after the sales most of the time. He was but little more of a mathematician than Ears, but he could count coconuts and read my list. If a man called for a stick of tobacco and a box of matches, Benny would be at a loss to estimate their combined price in coconuts, so I made it a rule that he should sell but one thing at a time. Thus he would count the eight coconuts and deliver the stick of tobacco, afterward counting the remaining two for the box of matches. When any one came into the store with money, he always called upon me lest the business should degenerate into the Ura One Pound Trading Company class.

I soon learned all the peculiarities of the Puka-Puka trade. Success depended upon stocking the store with articles of no earthly use to the islanders, avoiding everything that might have some intrinsic value. How like children my customers were! Why should they spend their money on umbrellas, or trousers, or tooth-brushes when they could buy toy balloons, pop-guns, and firecrackers.

But there surely was a run on talcum-powder; my entire supply of it was exhausted on the day the store opened, and six bottles of Shampoo d'Or were snapped up the second day. Perfume, too, was bought in large quantities and used internally, as medicine; but once I saw a village dandy pour a whole bottle of it over himself after his salt-water bath. Then he was off to the sea side of the islet, where, no doubt, he was highly successful in his love-making.

IV

The Kaupoe

Te vero ake nga o te ropa
Tupu i te wenua kaupoe.
Yala tona vaka
Tuki i te enemi—
Paf! Paf! Paf!
P'u te wui tane i te vave no te kaupoe.
Taki toru i te pitar'i,
I te rima kat'u,
I te rima k'ui,
Te rima ke—
E wakatoka pore koa varea
Nuti-nuti i te tino kiva.

In the land of the fearless cowboy
The youth grows tall and straight.
From his fleet canoe he shoots his enemies—
Paf! Paf! Paf!
Dead they all fall before him!
Three pistols has the cowboy,
One for the right hand,
One for the left hand,
And another—
Exultantly he doth despatch
All the fairest of the maidens.

—*From* "Mako Kaupoe" (*chant of the cowboy*), *composed by old William.*

The Kaupoe

"WHAT were you before you came to the islands?" old William asked one evening when a little group of men were gathered in the store.

It happened that I was thinking of ranching days, so I answered thoughtlessly, "A cowboy."

"A cowboy!" William cried.

"What! A cowboy?" shouted George.

The announcement created great excitement, for the myth of the American cowboy has even reached Puka-Puka. The few natives who have been to Rarotonga, Tahiti, or Apia have, of course, attended the cinemas there and brought back wonderful tales of cowboys. Island exhibitors have long since learned that Wild West movies are the big drawing-card, and the more bloodthirsty the picture, the larger the crowd. So the American cowboy is known, by report at least, all through the South Seas, even on such remote islands as Puka-Puka. He is regarded as a fierce, Indian-killing, seducing, stage-coach-robbing, reckless-riding hero, and among the islands nothing makes such a profound impression upon the natives as the admission that one has "cowboyed" now and then.

As a salve to my conscience I tried to explain to my admirers that a cowboy is really a quite ordinary person who takes care of cattle, driving them from one range to another, but old William, the much-traveled one, called me a liar, straight out.

"You can't fool me, Ropati-Cowboy!" he shouted. "Maybe you fool these goddam Kanakas, but gota-hell! You not fool me!" His great ears bobbed up

and down in his excitement. "Damn fool son-of-a-gun! Didn't Hosea that shipped to Apia with me tell how cowboys steal cattle? Ho, ho! Ropati-Cowboy! I savee too much. You not fool this old sailor, Ropati-Cowboy!"

William's line of profanity—Puka-Pukan, English, and even Spanish—is not particularly elegant, of course, but it is so much a part of the man that I can't leave all of it out if I am to show him as he is. His name for me, Ropati-Cowboy, took hold at once and to this day I have retained this honorable appellation. It adds more distinction than if I were to be called Sir Ropati or Lord Ropati, and infinitely more than such a title as Rev. Ropati, for like all healthy human animals, Puka-Pukans admire a sinful person.

Nothing would do, then, but that Aparo (Apollo), the island horse, must be brought, so that I might give an exhibition of my skill as a cowboy. The rest of the villagers, having been roused from their final evening slumbers, quickly gathered. Knowing that I would forever lose caste if I refused, I cut a few fathoms of rope, spliced a noose at one end, mounted the evil-eyed old nag, and kicked him into a stiff-legged trot. Taking a turn among the howling villagers, I cut out Ura, chief of police, from the crowd, dropped the noose over his head, and dragged him a few yards down the road, to the great delight of the spectators.

Having proved to their satisfaction that I was a cowboy, I dismounted and returned in triumph to the store.

II

My sins were turned against me that night. Having publicly shamed the chief of police by roping him, it was only fair that I should be roped in my turn, and so it happened: Maloko appeared on the scene. She walked shamelessly into my house, seated herself cross-legged on the floor, and proceeded to giggle. There are prettier girls on the island than Maloko, but she is far from plain—a little too rounded, perhaps, as to body, and with features not so regular as they might be, but on the whole not unattractive. I made use of my small vocabulary to ask what she wanted.

"To be your cook and housekeeper," she replied.

I was rather surprised at this; however, I nodded reflectively, gave her an appraising glance in search of the earmarks of a good cook, and although I found none, engaged her at once. I told her to come back in the morning and learn from Mama how to make coffee.

An expression of genuine concern came over her face. For a few moments she bent her head in thought as deep as her tiny brain was capable of. At length her face brightened and she replied: "No, if I am to be your cook and housekeeper, I shall sleep here."

Certainly there were prettier girls at Puka-Puka, and Maloko was approaching the dangerous age of eighteen, which is past the prime for Polynesian women; but at last I said: "All right. You may sleep on a mat in the corner." I went on to explain in a fatherly manner that it would be sinful to think of

any other arrangement: the church positively forbade it, and I could not even consider going against the dictates of the church.

"But aren't you a cowboy?" she asked.

Maloko had charm, no doubt, but I was still haunted by the firelight vision I had seen on my first night at Puka-Puka—and several times since as well—of a lovely little savage with a perfect olive skin, a bewitching oval face, and the slim body of a Diana. I explained as well as I could that cowboys are really very virtuous people and had little or nothing to do with women. If she insisted upon sleeping in my house, then she must be satisfied with a distant corner of the room, and on no condition was she to leave it. With that I blew out the light and crawled under my mosquito-net.

For some reason or other I slept restlessly that night. It may have been because I heard an occasional affected sigh from Maloko's corner, or because of a pernicious habit I have of enhancing the beauty of things when I hang them in my mental picture-gallery. However that may be, I tossed and turned for a long time before I fell into a light slumber.

I was awakened by some one shaking me by the shoulder.

"Ropati-Cowboy!" a voice whispered, "there are many mosquitoes to-night, and I have no net."

"Oh, well," I said, "all right."

I was really annoyed the next day when I found that Maloko had bragged through the three villages about how she had roped and tied the cowboy.

III

I was not long in learning the Puka-Puka language, for all the Polynesian tongues are allied, and already I had a fair knowledge of Tahitian, Rarotongan, and half a dozen other dialects of the Maori speech. In three months' time I could speak the language with considerable fluency, but for a year or more I had difficulty in following conversations between natives when they slurred their words or expressed themselves in obscure Puka-Pukan metaphors.

The chief difficulty was distinguishing between homonymous words which usually have a subtle analogy, such as the word *ara,* for example. It was Benny who first pointed out to me that this word means both to sin and to waken; "for," he explained, "is it not a sin to waken a person who is deep in slumber, and very likely in the midst of pleasant dreams?"

At times I read the Rarotongan Bible to retain my knowledge of that language; this practice also helped me with the local vernacular, drawing my attention to contrasts in word-building.

With Puka-Pukan acquired, there was little left to do, so I devoted myself to my books. I have been a bookworm since childhood, but it was only when I settled down to reading on Puka-Puka that I lost myself completely in the world of books. They seemed to become living creatures; their sharply contrasting personalities often materialized so vividly before me that I would find myself talking aloud with them. They possessed me completely; some of them filled me with terror because of my realization of the power they had over me—all of which is difficult to explain, unless it be to some other recluse who has lived, alone of his kind, with only books for companions.

The great stylists haunted me: Pepys, Casanova, Swinburne, Borrow, Mungo Park, John Stowe, Sterne, Dumas, Pierre Loti. One of Swinburne's poems, "Hendecasyllabics," ran through my head for weeks until I feared for my sanity. To this day when I repeat the lines:

> In the month of the long decline of roses
> I, beholding the summer dead before me,
> Set my face to the sea and journeyed silent,

I cannot, for the life of me, stop until I have reached the last line. And even then I find myself repeating it over and over, to waken at night with such lines as—

> Knew the fluttering wind, the fluttered foliage,
> Shaken fitfully, full of sound and shadow,

echoing and reëchoing in my mind.

It required many weeks to finish Pepys's "Diary," for if I read in it more than a half-hour at a time the book would open before me in my dreams, and I would read on the whole night through, my mind inventing gossip in Pepys's peculiar style.

Casanova and Borrow did not haunt me so much in dreams, but I would lose myself in "Lavengro" and the "Memoirs," becoming oblivious of existence itself, until Benny came tramping through the house to open the store, or Maloko diffidently shook me to say that coffee was ready, and with a start I would realize that my lamp had burned out and I was reading by daylight.

To-day I have a thousand carefully selected volumes on my shelves, the wonder of the natives, who, knowing no other book than the Bible, take it for granted that all my books are Bibles of a sort. A few of my more intelligent neighbors realize that some of these Bibles are different, containing, perhaps, stories of Jesus and Noah and Abraham which were not thought proper for Puka-Puka readers.

Sometimes I relate to them the Hellenic myths, the traditions of King Arthur, stories from the "Arabian

Nights," or one of Grimm's "Fairy Tales," explaining that one is from the old Bible of the Greeks and another from the Bible of the early Britons, etc., but my audiences are never convinced. When I have carefully explained the matter, some one is sure to ask, "But why was it left out of our Bible?" Then, more than likely, they will laugh and say: "Ah, Ropati-Cowboy, we know you! You are a sinful man who steals cattle and then says he is only driving them from one place to another! You can't fool us! All those books are Bibles!"

V

Little Sea

Na wakataka a taua rorona takiti,
Timo ko te ngaro ko te yu e wia e Ruka.
E kekema ko te maru awiawi,
Tu m'i koe peka roro taua kiwea
Kave ko te rangi ke ng'ong'o.

In the deepening twilight I will lead you
To a lonely secret place.
There no man's eye will see you;
We shall flee through curtaining clouds
And nest in the farthest heavens.

—*From* "Mako Koni-koni" (*a Puka-Pukan love chant*).

Little Sea

THE three villages on Puka-Puka are called Ngake, Roto, and Yato. The first means Windward, the second Central, and the third Leeward.

There are also three islets on the Danger Island reef, each village owning one. Central Village, being the sleepiest of the three, has contented itself with Puka-Puka Islet, the one from which the atoll derives its name. Central Village considers itself lucky in possessing this islet, for when the time comes for copra-making the villagers have only to go into their back yards to gather their nuts. But there is this drawback to such ownership: the other two villages also harvest many nuts there, for all three villages are situated on Puka-Puka Islet. Pirato-Ariki, the King of Puka-Puka, belongs to Central Village, but this has no political significance.

Leeward Village owns Frigate Bird Islet (Motu Kotaua). It is the smallest of the three but valuable because of the thousands of sea-birds that nest there. There is also a fine tract of guano, inland, where grow limes, oranges, breadfruit, and mummy-apples. Nearly every month the Leeward Villagers go to Frigate Bird Islet, scramble up the great puka-trees, and rob the nests of fat young sea-birds.

At first I would not eat a frigate bird, a booby, or a shearwater, but after a few months on the island I tried one broiled over coconut-shell coals, and I have never since missed an opportunity for such a feast. In a civilized country where one has an abundance of fresh meat the thought of a frigate-bird meal would, perhaps, be abhorrent; but on an atoll where the weekly chicken and the monthly pig make the sum total of fresh meat, an ancient man-of-war hawk seems as succulent as a squab would be at home.

The Leeward Villagers are by far the most hospitable of the Puka-Pukans, due, perhaps, to the fact that their islet is the poorest. They get even less copra than Central Village, despite that village's loss through the pilfering of its neighbors.

Windward Village owns the big islet of Ko, which produces more copra than the other two together; but there is little taro on Ko, and for some unaccountable reason the sea-birds shun it. Owing to their great wealth, which in English money may even exceed one pound sterling per capita per annum, they are inclined to be supercilious and patronizing toward their less wealthy neighbors. Nevertheless, there is a warm spot in my heart for Windward Village, for I have a snug little house resting on the point of their islet;

furthermore, Maloko, Little Sea, Desire, and Flame all belong to that settlement.

Puka-Puka is, perhaps, the only example on earth of a successful communistic government; and perhaps, also, this is due to the fact that no other community equals this one in sheer good-natured indolence. Here there is no private ownership of lands other than the tracts upon which the houses are built, and even in this case the land really belongs to the villages, which give the residents unlimited lease to live thereon.

When the villagers move for a few weeks' sojourn on their respective islets, the coconuts are gathered, stacked in the temporary village, and then equally divided among the men and women, a small share being reserved for the children. The nuts are then opened and the meat dried into copra, which is pooled and sold to my store or direct to Captain Viggo when he visits the island. The money received is either divided equally among the villagers or used to purchase clothing, tobacco, tin whistles, and firecrackers, which are divided. Likewise, when it is found that the puka-trees are full of young birds, the men catch them and the same division takes place. Even the fishing is often managed in this manner, as I shall describe later.

The general management of the work rests with the fathers of the village, who belong to an organization called "The Company" (Kamupani). They meet once a month or oftener to deliberate on community activities.

II

A Puka-Pukan's life history is divided into three periods: the Naked or *Takaua* period, the Mature or *Malo* period, and the Father or *Matua* period.

During the years of nakedness the child wanders through the groves in blessed indolence and ignorance, too young for the manly pastimes of shooting marbles or making string baskets. He takes his morning nap in the school-house, his afternoon siesta under the tamanu-trees on the sea side of the islet, and at evening he is fondled by the women, throws stones at roosting fowls, and whoops and yells as he splashes about in the lagoon shallows. The pre-missionary law was that no one under the age of eighteen should wear clothing; but the precise age is somewhat doubtful, for my neighbor Bones says that it was twenty-five when he was a child, and furthermore, that the fathers at one time decided that even this age was too early for the wearing of clothing. Therefore, instead of raising the age limit, they lengthened the year, making it fifteen moons long instead of twelve. In those days, as today, permission to wear clothing was a tacit admission that the child was old enough to look upon the opposite sex. The only serious employment permitted to children of the naked age is to fish in the lagoon, but this means little, for I have yet to see one of these naked youngsters able to concentrate his energy long enough to fish.

When a child reaches the proper age he is officially "Made-into-a-man" (Akatane). At a meeting of the village fathers he is proclaimed as being old enough to enter into the village work, fish outside the reef, and to turn his eyes toward the ladies. This is a great day for him. A pig is killed, much taro cooked, and at night he slips bashfully to the lonely outer beach where the youngsters convene, there to choose a sweetheart. He has become *malo*. The word means mature, hard, fierce, fecund, and is the name of a kind of sennit rope which is wrapped around the body twenty or thirty times as a belt. In the old days the coming of age was ceremonialized by binding the *malo* about the youth. It was the first clothing of any sort he was permitted to wear.

At the age of fifty a Puka-Pukan retires from manual labor and becomes one of the members of The Company, spending his evenings shooting popguns or playing checkers, and his nights in ordering the young fry about. He never again has to go fishing, to gather coconuts, or to do any other work. When the *malos* bring in their fish they are given to the fathers, who divide them after picking out the choice bits for themselves. Other food is handled in a similar manner. To be sure, many of the fathers spend a day or two at fishing now and then, but this is not required of them and they do it only to pass the time; and the fish they catch are their own, while those of the *malos* belong to the community.

So it goes. Such a life would be unutterably monotonous for high-strung, wealth-loving Europeans or Americans, but it suits the easy-going Puka-Pukans to a T. Of course, if they had the slightest taint of ambition their system would fail, for under it it is quite impossible for one man to be richer than his neighbor. When, in the course of decades or generations, some unnatural "go-getter" happens to be born, he soon finds life so intolerable that he emigrates to an island where communism doesn't prevail. But Puka-Pukans, with very few exceptions, are wholly satisfied with their system. They avoid all land disputes, and no one is faced with the problem of how to make a better appearance in the world than his neighbor. The young sparks can let off steam as George did on the night of my arrival, and older men who are inclined to be ambitious can become a power in The Company as King-of-the--Sky has become. It is always possible for a young and lusty man to have a violent love affair with his neighbor's daughters, thus gaining distinction in a manner the Puka-Pukan appreciates.

III

Three or four weeks after my arrival on Puka-Puka the natives decided to go to their respective islets to make copra. I awoke one morning to find that the villagers too were awake, or, rather, had forborne going to sleep, and when Maloko called me for coffee the lagoon was dotted with half a hundred sailing canoes.

All the settlements were deserted, and while I was breakfasting Benny came to me to explain that he could not work in the store during the coming month because it was the law of the island that every man, woman, and child must go to their islets, or, as was the case with Central Village, go to their temporary village on the sea side of Puka-Puka Islet. Benny also hinted that it would be proper for me to go to Ko, for I belonged to Windward Village, now that I had a mistress from that settlement.

By the time I had finished coffee I had decided to go, but I had no intention of taking Maloko with me. I went into the store, cut a few yards of muslin dress goods, packed a box with food, rolled up my blankets, pillow, and mosquito-net, and told Benny to put a sail on the canoe. Half an hour later I was skimming across the lagoon, alone. I had disloyally abandoned my cook and housekeeper.

Steering for the northwest point of Ko, called Matauea, I dodged among the coral heads until a gust of wind drove the canoe on to the pure white sand of the Point. One little coconut-frond house was there, occupied by Sea Foam and his family. The worthy preacher met me on the beach and invited me to stay with him. I had counted on this and carried my things into the house. The box of provisions I put at his disposal, first securing and hiding the parcel containing the muslin dress.

On the western side of Matauea Point is a half-mile stretch of shallow water, where at low tide are large exposed tracts of salmon-colored coral as flat as a table and broken by shallow basins filled with six or eight inches of tepid water where the fish find refuge until the next tide. On the northern and eastern sides of the Point are beaches of coral sand shelving steep-to into water about ten fathoms deep. This makes an ideal swimming place; and, better still, one can throw a line from the bank and catch a morning's breakfast without greatly exerting one's self. Fine rock grouper are caught there, and every now and then a young jack, a milk mullet, or a red-snapper will take the hook. The trade wind blows refreshingly cool across the Point, clearing it of mosquitoes and singing an eternal psalm in the fronds of the coconut-palms. It is a beautiful spot, and I have often fancied that when my trading days are over I would build a comfortable house on Matauea Point, devoting the rest of my days to a hedonistic, pagan life: fishing, falling to sleep among the volumes of a picaresque library, dreaming at times of the delirious, turbulent world I once knew, and happily, so far away; and again at times loving some island woman with the clear-eyed appreciative passion of an old man. It would be a fitting way for an island trader to end his days; and when he closed his eyes for the last time and he was snugly buried in the clean coral sand, how well he would sleep there, the trade-wind rocking the palms over his grave and the long Pacific rollers thundering along the reef off-shore.

IV

When night was descending softly over the groves I secreted the muslin dress under my shirt, told Sea Foam I was going for a stroll, and hurried down the path leading to Windward Village's Ko settlement. Sea Foam's face had lengthened in true missionary fashion—his wife was regarding him at the time, and it is the duty, of course, of all island brethren-of-the-

Lord to show suspicion when young men take night promenades. Suspicion is as much a part of the preacher's business as the night walk is a part of the young man's. But as I turned to go I thought I detected the hint of a smile on Sea Foam's rugged face.

Half-way to the copra-maker's settlement I stopped abruptly. I was wet with perspiration, and I felt that I must wait till the fire in my brain had subsided. I had been walking rapidly, staring at a vision far ahead, a vision of youth and passion I had carried with me from the night of my arrival at Puka-Puka. A long reach of moonlight had broken through the trees to melt into the damp trembling green of the jungle growth. The islet seemed to pant like a lustful tigress, her breath pregnant with redolent odors of a heavy Oriental fragrance. Of a sudden I understood: all this land and sea, dormant by day, had awakened at dusk, refreshed, hungry, carnal, to lie with damp breasts bare for her lover, Night, descending slowly, passionately, inexorably. I hurried on.

I found her before one of the first houses in the settlement. A tattered dress fell about her shoulders and her face was almost hidden in a great mass of loose hair as she leaned over her task of grating coconuts. An old crone and a man with elephantiasis legs were sitting near-by taking turns in puffing at a pandanus-leaf cigarette. They grinned, bobbed their heads in greeting, and then gave all their attention to the precious cigarette.

"What a little Cinderella!" I thought, moving toward the firelight vision. "Although we can't conjure up a pumpkin coach, there is at least a prince bearing gifts of muslin at your service."

She left off her work with a smile as I sat down beside her, and listened seriously when I started talking foolishness. When the old people's heads were turned I whispered a suggestion that we should walk through the groves to the sea side of the islet and go swimming in a moonlit pool of the shallows. But there was no need for caution; she jumped to her feet, announced that she was going walking with the white man, and ran into the hut.

While she was gone another girl

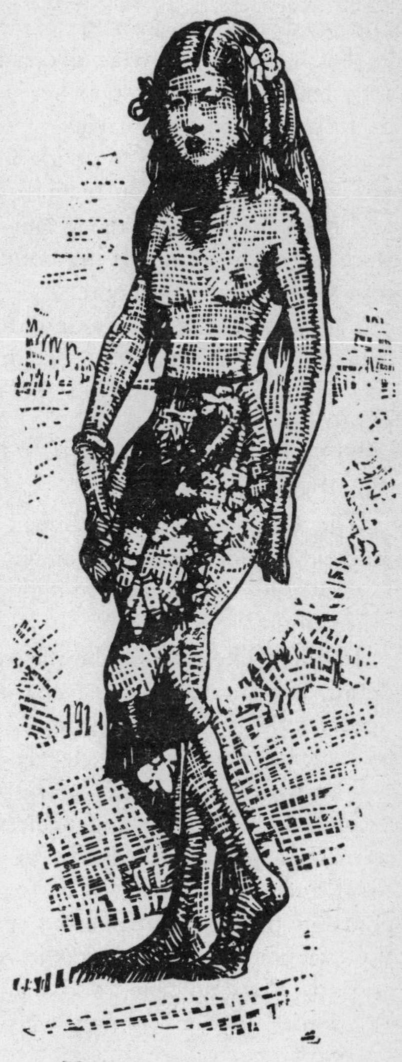

appeared and she seemed to me almost as beautiful as Little Sea. She was dressed in a short skirt of fern leaves wound around her waist and appeared to be fully aware of her ravishing form. Her black eyes wandered over me in a wondering way; her nose was almost Aryan, her mouth small, and her hair straight and black like an Indian's. But what I most admired were the smooth lines of her body just metamorphosing into those of womanhood.

Presently Little Sea came out of the house dressed in a red and white *pareu,* and her hair, scented with coconut oil, shimmering in the moonlight. She was ready for the promenade.

"This is my cousin, Desire" (Inangaro), she said. "Shall she come with us?"

The muslin dress had slipped down. I hesitated a moment while I tucked it under my arm again. Then I answered: "No, not to-night, but certainly some other night."

I should like to describe the events of that night in detail, but for various reasons it will be best to pass lightly over them; furthermore, I was too intoxicated to remember everything clearly.

The wide outer beach sparkled beneath the moon, a couch fit for any island princess. The reef combers seemed to grumble jealously as they leaned over the coral and lost themselves in foaming phosphorescent pools in the lagoon. The water was as clear as the sky; we could see the fantastic coral shapes and their myriad colors, softened and shaded by the moonlight. We waded in—it was only waist-deep—and splashed about like four-year-old babies; and later we dried our bodies by racing along the sand, dancing, and singing. Then, lying on the beach, Little Sea pointed out the stars, told me their native names and some quaint little legends about them. The Milky Way was the Shark, Venus was *Rupe-rupe,* a dove, the Southern Cross was a bird, and the Magellanic clouds were Mr. North Wind and Mrs. South Wind, and there was a somewhat improper allusion in the story which the reader can inquire into when he comes to Puka-Puka.

Before returning we did all kinds of foolish things; among others I taught her how to kiss in the civilized manner, for she knew only the calflike rubbing of noses and sniffing. But when she had mastered the civilized art, she in turn became teacher, giving me lessons in the native *ongi-ongi* (smelling).

I asked her to live with me when we returned to the main islet.

"Oh, I should be very much ashamed," she said with a note of real concern.

"I suppose you think it is wrong," I said, "to live with a white man unless you are married to him."

She laughed softly. "Oh, no, it isn't that. I should be ashamed because of Maloko, who is living with you now. She is my cousin."

"Well," I replied, "Maloko shall leave just as soon as I return. She is only my servant. I didn't ask her to come, but I shall tell her to go away."

"Aué te akaloa!" Little Sea sympathized with Maloko. As she turned, the light fell in enchanting shad-

ows across her face. Suddenly she forgot all about Maloko and started playing with my ears, for she had seen them wiggle during my vigorous remarks about Maloko. Being an expert at the art, I wiggled my ears a hundred times, greatly to her delight. She thought it a wonderful accomplishment. A moment or two later her head sank on my arm, and I was surprised to find that she was asleep.

Toward midnight, when we were approaching her hut, I gave her the muslin dress. She refused at first, then accepted it reluctantly, as though afraid that otherwise I would be angry. A moment later she ran into the hut, the dress hidden in the folds of her *pareu.*

I sat for a while under a tree where the shadows were deep, watching the house in true lover fashion. I was rewarded at length, for Little Sea came out again and kindled a fire before the door. Then Desire appeared and leaning closely together the two girls talked for a long time. Little Sea was telling her cousin all about it.

VI

The Young Unmarried

Toku tamaiti reka taiao,
P'u te ka waro i te maro.
Ivi pakari, kiko makeke;
Kii i te awi no te Kaki.

This day my son is happy,
The long sennit is wrapped about him.
His bones are hard, his flesh is solid;
The passion of the Kaki has seized him.

—*From* "Mako Kaki" (*chant of the young unmarried*).

The Young Unmarried

ON returning from Ko, I found Maloko waiting patiently. She had heard about my affair with Little Sea, but she took my unfaithfulness philosophically, as though it were no more than one should expect from a man.

I was wondering just what I should do about Maloko, when I was saved from my embarrassing position by Ura, chief of police and sometimes deacon of the church, who came with his three assistant policemen, Ears (Taringa), Husks (Puru), and Everything (Katoa), to tell me that Maloko was a married woman and that I was breaking the law of the island as well as of the Lord by keeping her.

Ears, the Leeward policeman, Husks, the one from Central Village, and Everything, the guardian from Windward Village, stood behind little five-foot Ura, nodding their heads gravely.

Ura smiled foxily, decorating his speech with apostrophes of the most flattering nature, for he seemed concerned lest he should anger me and equally concerned lest I refuse to give up Maloko.

"I would not bother you," he explained, "about so unimportant a thing as a woman; but the difficulty is that her husband came to me yesterday and demanded that I find her. I did not tell him where she was. I merely said that she must have been strolling through the villages the past few months and had forgotten to go home. That was a clever speech of mine, for, excepting yourself, of course, I am the cleverest man on Puka-Puka. . . . Ah, a stick of tobacco! Thank you, Ropati-Cowboy, thank you! My three humble policemen also thank you." At this he flourished his stumpy arm toward his henchmen, forgetting, however, to share the tobacco with them.

Then, with a mealy-mouthed leer, he concluded: "And now, Ropati-Cowboy, if you will permit, I and my policemen will take Maloko back to her husband and nobody will be the wiser."

I was amused by the shamelessness, the obsequiousness, and the barefaced lying of the little cop, and I was more than pleased to think that I should so easily get rid of Maloko.

At that moment she herself appeared, hurling scathing invectives at each of the policemen in turn. With a majestic wave of his hand and a soapy grimace at me, Everything stepped forward, seized Maloko, and dragged her out of the store, while she bawled like a school-girl.

I felt genuinely sorry for my late mistress. Picking up a *pareu,* a tin of beef, and several other things, I ran after the police force and thrust them into Maloko's arms. She dried her tears at once like a child when it receives the stick of candy it has been crying for. She smiled sweetly, tucked the valuables under her arm, gave me a flirtatious glance, stuck out her tongue at the chief of police, and peacefully followed Everything to her expectant husband.

I do not wish to give a false impression concerning the morals of the Puka-Pukans. Adultery is practically unknown on the island. Before the young people marry they are given what amounts to unlimited freedom to find temporary mates. I believe that they become sated with sex when young, leaving them with no desire for amorous adventures in middle life. The system works well here, but would not do, of course, in a country where malignant diseases are common. Maloko was an exception. She had been forced into marriage when very young—about twelve, I believe—by parents who had the more civilized notion of morals. She soon left her husband and went on a sex spree, for hers was no love match, and she had been cheated of her period of the usual sexual abandonment to which every young Puka-Pukan looks forward as a natural right. From that time on she had lived intermittently with her husband.

Maloko and I are good friends to this day. She has grown fat, and is as cheerful and care-free as ever, and has a large progeny by a new spouse.

II

At night there are shadows in the coconut-groves

of Puka-Puka—lacelike shadows of fronds, shadows of stiff-limbed pandanus-trees, of ground bush, and of the fleecy trade-wind clouds skimming low overhead. And there are the shadows of the young unmarried, wide awake now and slipping from tree to tree on their way to the love fests on the sea side of the islet.

One night not long after Maloko was persuaded to return to her husband, I crossed the causeway to Leeward Village and followed the outer beach where stretches of coral sand glimmer faintly under the light of stars and moon.

Presently I came to a spot where the young unmarried were gathered. A plaintive heathen strain sounded from a copse of bush; farther on some one was drumming a weird rhythm on a coconut-shell while a girl and a boy danced before him. I could hear laughing cries from out on the reef and see shadowy figures here and there.

I cannot speak of all that I saw: it is enough to say that there were no spying chaperons, spoil-sports, or moralizing parents to hinder the wild youth in their adventures or to prevent them from understanding one another as God must have meant them to. If there is any place on earth where men and women live naturally, surely it is on Puka-Puka.

Later, when a white resident agent came to the island, he tried to put a stop to the love-making on the outer beach. I immediately pleaded with him for "flaming youth," pointing out the fact that it is not in the nature of the Polynesian to control himself in such matters. I also tried to convince him that if he prohibited free love among the young people, they would either turn to perverse practices or break the law, either of which would be worse than the present state of affairs. I urged that the Puka-Puka love fests are of great antiquity and cause no harm whatever on an island where there are no diseases to be transmitted and where unmarried mothers lose no social standing.

But the resident agent was new to the islands and a believer in a London missionary society code of ethics for primitive Polynesians. However, in the end he gave in; there was nothing else for him to do.

I am convinced that the freedom of the young people of Puka-Puka between the ages of fourteen and eighteen is the direct cause of their fidelity after they have selected permanent mates. They have unlimited opportunity to become intimately acquainted with each other, thus lessening the possibility of post-connubial disillusionment.

Until within a few years of my arrival on Puka-Puka it had been the custom for boys and girls to don their first grass skirt or pandanus loin-cloth upon joining the love fests. Marriage, as well as other sexual relations, was prohibited to males under eighteen and females under fifteen. The punishment for disobedience was months of hard labor digging out taro-beds, a punishment sufficiently severe to create a deep respect for the law. If an outraged father caught his fourteen-year-old daughter demurely donning a grass skirt, he would tear it from her and cuff her ears soundly; likewise, if a seventeen-year-old buck arrayed himself in a sennit belt, he was dealt with as the circumstances demanded, for to allow him to dress would be a tacit admission that he was old enough to join the love-making classes on the outer beach.

But upon reaching the legal age, clothing was given them: a valance-like piece of matting for the men, bound around their waists with the belt of sennit already described, and a bushy frond skirt for the girls. They were then permitted to "sin" before marriage. All of this was a wise procedure, for it kept the young people from sexual indulgence until they had reached maturity, and so they grew to be a strong race. Their nakedness did not excite salacious thoughts, for it is well known to all those who have lived among savages, excepting only the missionaries, who refuse to be enlightened, that nakedness tends to allay sexual passion, while clothing aggravates it by exciting the imagination.

Nowadays the missionaries, in a strangely myopic and blundering fashion, have unwittingly reduced the age limit for girls to twelve years, and for boys to thirteen, for they insist on their being clothed at these ages. It would be impossible to convince them that by so doing they are promoting lechery instead of preventing it, for they accept no traditions but their borrowed Hebrew ones. This is nevertheless the case, for the simple-minded Puka-Pukans, who for ages have looked upon the wearing of clothing as an admission to sexual rights, consider that the authorization of trousers and skirts for their children at the same time authorizes them to wander to the sea side of the islet on moonlight nights.

Clothes! Clothes! Clothes! The missionaries are obsessed by the thought of clothes, sincere, good-hearted folk though many of them are. Longer skirts, longer sleeves, higher necks for the women's dresses! "Cover up the sinful body!" is the text of most of their sermons. A South Sea trader should not complain, I suppose, for the more clothing, the more copra; nevertheless, the whole business grates on me, and I would rather do less trading and see my neighbors return to more healthful habits of life.

The sun had just set behind the trees of Yato Point and the cloud-reflected light lay softly on the schoolhouse across the road, when one of the wild youth of Leeward Village poked his head in the doorway and beckoned me to come outside. His name was Rori (Sea Cucumber), but when I addressed him by this name he shook his head and said, "My name is not Rori. You must have some one else in mind. I am called Mr. Chair."

Then with many mysterious nods and grimaces he grasped my arm and urged me to come with him. My curiosity was soon aroused and I followed him briskly.

When we came to Husks's house he stopped, and assuming a lackadaisical attitude stared vacantly down the road, apparently not aware that Husks's three fair daughters were gazing at us curiously. With an offhand, fribbling air he made a sign with his hand in such a way that an onlooker would have thought nothing of it, but it had deep significance for the three maidens.

Then he swung his right hand in a circle with all five fingers outspread; next his left hand with only three fingers showing. Then he clapped his hands and raised them to his shoulders in a motion which, to the initiated, might indicate the act of throwing water over the body in bathing. Finally he swung his right hand up and down as one would do in beating a tom-tom, and with that he again grasped my arm and we walked on.

When we had gone some little distance he explained that these were the signals of his secret society. His pantomime meant "Five girls and three girls meet five boys and three boys at the fresh-water bathing tank when the curfew tom-tom sounds."

"They count them up on their fingers," Mr. Chair went on. "Five and three are eight. So eight of them will come, one for each of us."

"Us!" I said. "Am I to be one of the party?"

"Yes," he replied; "we have decided to take you into our society. You must meet us at the government tank when the curfew sounds. Your new name will be Mr. Cigarette."

When Husks sounded the curfew—a ceremony that had no significance whatever on Puka-Puka except that it was following out the Rev. Mr. Johns's orders—I laid down my book, tied a colored handkerchief around my neck, and went to the bathing tank. There, lurking in the shadows of adjacent trees, were seven youths from Leeward Village and eight maidens from

Central Village. In honor of myself, the new member of the society, they were dressed in all their finery, but on future occasions they would wear their more attractive grass skirts and *pareus*.

Mr. Chair stepped forward to introduce me—to the men first. There was Mr. Thread, a tall slim youth wearing his father's No. 11 shoes. We rubbed noses. Then came Mr. Guitar, Mr. Horse, Mr. Undershirt, Mr. Bull, and Mr. Coconut. I was presented to each of them as the new member from Cowboyland, Mr. Cigarette by name.

I realized that in this ceremony our real names were taboo. It was a taboo similar to that of the Samoan bonito fishermen, who, when after this kingly fish, will never call an eye an eye but must give it some other name. Similarly, the parts of the body, the canoe, and fishing gear—the very act of paddling—have special names in this language of courtesy.

I was then introduced to the young ladies. They were all between the ages of fourteen and eighteen, and, like most Polynesian girls, were very pretty. But what an evanescent beauty! Eight years hence many of them would be middle-aged if not old women. "Sweet little sisterhood," I thought. "Let them taste of the honey of love while they may, for their flowers will soon fade."

I was first presented to Miss Laughter and was delighted to rub noses with her. Then came Miss Ribbon, Miss Bird, Miss Chemise, Miss Handkerchief, Miss Perfume, and Miss Redfish.

"And this, Mr. Cigarette," said Mr. Chair, "is your gift-woman (*yana-wawine*) for to-night. She is called Miss Button."

I took Miss Button by the arm, delighted to see that she was more simply dressed than the others, in a red and white *pareu* and a wreath of gardenias. We followed the other members of the society, reaching the outer beach just as the yellow moon, three-quarters full, rose above the sea. And now, I think, the time has come to bring to a close my story of Mr. Chair's secret society.

There is a world of interesting lore concerning these love fests, and, of course, I consented to join them only for scientific reasons, so that I might study more intimately ancient Puka-Puka customs. But in all seriousness I can say that in many respects they partake of the nature of religious ceremonies. Could anthropologists study these rituals—in a strictly platonic manner—much would be found in them dating undoubtedly from times immemorial, and perhaps light would be shed on other mysteries of Polynesian origin. Although I have speculated on these matters, I will not record my erudite conclusions, for these memoirs are in too light a vein to admit of anthropological conclusions reached through frequenting Puka-Pukan saturnalias.

A vision I had already had of Aphrodite unveiled made me wonder how much longer it would be before Little Sea was initiated into one of these outer-beach societies. I did not relish the thought of her doing so before becoming mine. Although I thoroughly sanctioned the love fests for young Puka-Pukans, a white man of necessity labors under the heritage of his blood: jealousy is bred into him through countless generations of men for whom chastity was a social necessity. With the natives it is but a momentary passion and not a very violent one at that. After thinking matters over I decided to keep Little Sea from joining the others by making her my mistress and, perhaps, eventually my wife.

VII

Mr. and Mrs. Turtle

Liaki pae, pae i raro ko te tauanga!
Na pukea e te pou tini-tini,
Na wai ki te vave o te tangata.
Ko te ika lele na te wui ropa,
Na kapi i runga, na kapi i raro.
Tautau na wui kaokao.
Ekiai na toka te kai tangi.
Tuki! Pate!
Pate mai runga!
Vavaji ake!

The young men have caught a great turtle,
The warriors, the men of our village!
They hold him secure in their strong hands
While I wield the knife that will kill him.
Oh, he is fat from his back to his belly!
Oh, he is fat from his head to his tail!
We of the village are hungry.
Baste him one! Whack him!
Batter his back!
Cleave him in two!

—*From* "Mako Onu" (*turtle-hunters' chant.*)

Mr. and Mrs. Turtle

THE day was breathlessly hot. Ura, chief of police, steamed and sweated as he lolled from one door of his coral-lime house to the other in a vain attempt to intercept the ghost of a breeze. At length he abandoned the hope of finding comfort indoors, and sent his numerous children in search of Ears, Husks, and Everything.

In the course of time the three policemen appeared, and having consulted with their chief, they went off to their respective villages to cry the law of Ura: every man, woman, and child was to go to the outer beach for a grand community turtle-hunt.

I was sitting on the front balcony above the trading-station when Husks announced the coming event at Central Village. Men and women rose from their morning slumber to stagger out into the blazing sunlight. They blinked stupidly, rolled their tongues in their cheeks, scratched their heads, and still half asleep, turned to cross the islet to the outer reef.

Hitching up my *pareu* and hanging a pair of water goggles around my neck, I followed.

Community fishing is a common occurrence on Puka-Puka. Periodically, one of the villages rouses itself and issues a challenge to the other two to join in a fishing competition for rock grouper, snappers, bonito, albacore, flying-fish, turtle, or whatever kind of fish happens to be plentiful at the time. When the day's fishing is over, each participant takes his catch to the churchyard, where it is counted and scored for his village. The village scoring the largest combined catch is entitled to do a little song and dance, usually very wicked, in which many disparaging allusions are made concerning the members of the losing villages. Then the fish are divided equally among all the men, women and children of the island. Every one hugely enjoys these competitions, even saturnine old William, who roars out curses and cynical remarks with greater gusto than usual. Then the people go home to cook their fish, none too fragrant after a day in the full blaze of the Puka-Puka sun.

Ura, being chief of police, could not, of course, lower his dignity by opening any trifling competition such as a grouper-fishing where there would not be the slightest risk of any one being killed or maimed for life. With him it must be torchlight netting along the treacherous sunken *Arai* reef, or best of all because most dangerous, turtle-hunting. Although little Ura could not possibly bring in a turtle, he could at least send out his neighbors to hazard their lives, and personally accept the credit for a big catch.

Benny overtook me before I reached the reef. He was carrying a piece of light native wood about four feet long and six inches wide. It was for me, he explained, to be used as a head-rest while at sea, so that if I wanted to I could take my usual siesta.

On reaching the outer reef I was startled at the sight of the gigantic combers roaring along the serrations and knife-edges of coral, but Benny was not in the least alarmed. He flung my board beyond the breakers and without waiting for a lull ran confidently out to the spot where an immense comber was just curling to fall. In another instant he would have been crushed to death on the coral had he not plunged headlong into the foam. I lost sight of him for half a minute, but presently he bobbed up beyond the breakers, smiling, and as happy as a porpoise.

I knew how he had done it, having seen the same thing done many times before, but I had never had the courage to attempt it myself. Benny had merely hurried out between breakers to a point where the undertow would carry him to sea, although the foam above him was rushing shoreward. After swimming with the undertow until nearly out of breath, he had brought himself to the surface with a few strong strokes.

While hesitating, I heard a cackling voice cry: "Come on, Ropati-Cowboy!" It was old Mama. She hobbled industriously past, her breath coming short and raspingly. As unconcernedly as Benny she made her way across the reef, her grass skirt but partially hiding her fleshless limbs, and her shoulder bones protruding as sharply as juts of coral underfoot.

"Lord!" I wondered, "will Little Sea ever be like that?"

Just then, with an indecorous flutter of grass skirts, old Mama flopped into a billow of foam and a moment later reappeared far beyond the break of the surf.

I hesitated no longer, for I thought I saw Little Sea and her cousin Desire out beyond Benny, and I wondered whether they were laughing at me. I rushed out, threw myself into the next comber with suicidal abandon, and dived until my hands touched the coral. Then, to my astonishment—for I expected only to make myself ridiculous—I found that I was being carried rapidly seaward. The foam thinned, disappeared, and, as I was wearing my water goggles, I could pilot myself through the fantastic forests of coral. There were mountains that seemed to be standing upside down, canyons wider at the base than at the top, dark caves from which slimy things stared, coral trees whose roots were spread out in the water while their boughs were embedded deep in the sea, bottomless abysses, and colors such as we poor humans who live on land never dream of. A huge fish finned lazily only a few feet away, and a shark eyed me as he swam gravely past.

On crossing a crevice in the coral I saw the head of a conger-eel, his cold bloodless eyes watching me as though deliberating whether or not to attempt such a large morsel. His fang-toothed mouth was quite large enough to have taken my leg. I had heard of men being seized by giant keptocephali and held beneath the surface until they drowned. Panic seized me and I swam frantically for the surface. Then of a sudden my fears vanished, for there was Benny at my side, grinning reassuringly. He had come down to see to it that nothing happened to the boss of his store. My confidence returned at once; I felt that I could have returned and kicked that conger-eel out of his hole.

"Ah!" said Benny with one of his usual "ifs" when we had reached the surface, "if you had followed Mama you would have seen something! There was a whooper of a shark here just now."

The long swells and the wide hollows between them were dotted with heads, for most of the inhabitants of Puka-Puka had come out. Little Ura, with a gorgeous red and yellow *pareu* about his loins, was chattering away, ordering the young men of his village to catch many turtles for the honor of the sometimes

deacon of the church. Mama was by no means the only grandma present, for the octogenarians had turned out *en masse* from their huts and lean-tos and were paddling about, diving and splashing as unconcernedly as though they really belonged in the sea rather than on land. Some of them were buoyed up with pieces of wood such as mine, and they were so completely at home in the water that they actually dozed off for a few minutes from time to time, resting on their little supports.

On the other islands, Penrhyn and Manihiki for example, there would have been much concern about sharks, but at Puka-Puka no one pays the slightest attention to them. It is claimed that no one of the island has ever been attacked by a shark, and I know from experience that they treat these monsters with complete indifference.

Benny and I swam leisurely along the reef. With our water goggles adjusted we gazed at the fishes displaying their polychromatic scales to the sea world, as, with true Puka-Pukan languor, they finned from coral to coral. As the current carried us along, I saw, in a fissure in the sloping bottom, a great *patuki,* his body partially hidden, but his immense fanged jaws in full view. The brute was not over eight feet long, but his mouth was large enough to swallow two men at once. He was mostly head, his body tapering to a cone. It made me decidedly uncomfortable to think that, if he caught a man, he would have to digest half of him before the other half could enter his stomach, much like a frog dining on a sparrow. And if he caught him feet first, and the man's head reached above the surface—well, it would be anything but a pleasant sort of death.

Benny too saw the monster. "That is the only fish the Puka-Pukans fear," he said. "Look at his mouth! Big enough to swallow a man!"

With a painful attempt at nonchalance I replied: "Yes, but his body is not big enough to hold half a man, so we have nothing to fear."

Just then the *patuki* wriggled out of his hole and opening his jaws in a blood-curdling manner, displayed a saber-toothed mouth and a blood-red gullet.

Benny was unawed. "That's right," he said. "I never thought of that. There is nothing to fear."

With that he turned head downward with a duck-like flop, swam close to the monster, and gave him a contemptuous kick. The *patuki* closed his jaws with a snap and returned to his hole at once.

Benny's face was beaming when his head broke water. "Now I know that you were right when you said he was harmless!"

"And supposing I had been mistaken? What then?"

His face became grave at once. "I never thought of that!" he said. "If you had been mistaken he would have eaten me, wouldn't he?"

"Of course."

"You white men always think of these things; but they never occur to us Puka-Pukans. Anyway, now I have kicked one, I shall never be as afraid of *patuki* as I was before." He felt quite heroic when I explained to him the nature of his risk.

He then suggested that we swim a mile or two out to sea and hunt for a giant turtle. As is commonly known, these green turtles found in tropic seas live for a thousand years and weigh three or four hundred pounds. They have jaws capable of snapping off a man's arm with the ease of a shark bisecting a jelly-fish. But it is not commonly known, I believe, that the tails—of the males only—are their most deadly weapons.

Benny explained this to me as we swam leisurely seaward. The male's tail is much longer than the female's, and he has the habit of hooking it around anything that touches it, holding it in a vicelike grip, and sounding. So, when a man is grappling one of the giant Chelonia, if he allows his arm or leg to touch the tail, he is instantly caught, the tail hooking the limb and pinning it against the shell. Thereupon he loses his hold on the turtle's flipper while vainly trying to free himself, and is dragged beneath the surface to drown. For this reason the man who, alone, brings in a male turtle is looked upon as a *Toa* (a superman) by the people of the atolls.

A mile from shore we rested for a little while, propped up on my wooden support. The water was like polished steel, and now we were far enough from the reef to be in the midst of the great undulations of the Pacific. When we sank into the long troughs the island would be lost to view below the oily backs of the rollers, and then it required but little imagination to believe one's self hundreds of miles from land. But the next undulation would raise us, showing the island ablaze in the sunlight, an emerald of dazzling beauty resting lightly on the bosom of the sea. Benny was explaining the methods of catching the giant turtle.

"The easiest way is the most dangerous. You grasp the turtle by the skin at the nape of his neck, and then steer him ashore, riding on his back. This is seldom done with the male turtle, for your legs come too close to his tail. If we find a female turtle to-day you can ride her in this manner, but if it is a male, leave him to me. We hold the papa turtle by getting the right arm under his left front flipper; then, reaching up, we can catch hold of the front edge of his upper shell. This too is dangerous, because during the struggle the hands may come within reach of the turtle's mouth. That is how King Pirato's father was killed: the turtle grabbed him, carried him down, and drowned him. In either of these ways, once you have gotten a safe hold, the turtle cannot sound, and, since he is very clumsy, you can easily guide him by jerking him to one side or the other. Now, Ropati, you take the mama turtle and I will take her husband. Ura will be surprised when he sees us coming in."

"But hadn't we better find the turtles first?"

"There they are," said Benny. "I saw them a long time ago, but being a white man, you are not supposed to notice such things."

Following his gaze, I saw what appeared to be two coconuts floating a hundred yards or so away.

"Grab her like this," said Benny, taking me by the scruff of the neck, "and steer her this way." He jerked me from side to side in a most unceremonious manner. "Swim close behind and take the one I leave. We can surprise them, because they are in the midst of their love-making and are blind to everything else."

We swam to within twenty feet of them, adjusted our water goggles, and dived, Benny first, I following. They made a motion to part, when, in a flash, Benny twisted his arm around the larger turtle's left flipper. Instantly I lost them in a cloud of foam. I swam past, too excited to think of fear. The female was sounding, but her movements were so slow that I soon caught up with her. Following Benny's directions, I caught her by the nape, wound my legs around her shell, and pulled upward. She responded immediately, flapping to the surface in a panic, and just in time, too, for my lungs were bursting for want of air.

By the time I had overcome my excitement sufficiently to be aware of what I was doing I found my pelagic Pegasus swimming mightily for the coast of South America, many thousands of miles away. I had lost my board, and at the moment I could see neither Benny nor the island, as they were behind me; and here was I in the middle of the Pacific aboard a brute I was afraid either to turn loose or to stay on. I was helpless and was about to loosen my hold, when I heard Benny yelling Puka-Pukan curses behind me. He was telling me to turn the creature landward. For the moment I had forgotten his instructions about guiding; now, putting them in practice, my fiery turtle turned like a well-broken mare. A moment later, rising to the top of a swell, I saw the island before me, and Benny, all submerged but his head, driving his papa turtle toward the reef.

The male turtle was swifter than the female, reaching the reef in about thirty minutes, while my Chelonia needed a good three-quarters of an hour, so Benny had his safely turned over before I arrived. I was glad, for I enjoyed the glory of coming in alone, and when, about two hundred yards from the reef, I met Little Sea and Desire—pretty little water nymphs—I lost six points in my course while gazing at them.

"*Aué!* Have you got a turtle?" cried Little Sea.

I was as offhand about it as possible, saying that old Mama had been pestering me for turtle steak, so I had to go out and get her some.

"*Aué!* The white man's got a big turtle!" little Desire screamed, and the words were as welcome to me as honey to a bear. They swam beside me, one on either side, and no returning Roman conqueror could have ridden the high horse with more vainglory than I rode my lowly Mrs. Turtle. As we approached the reef, however, I had grave doubts as to how my triumph would end. I now knew how to get out to sea but had not the faintest notion of how to weather the surf in getting ashore. But with Little Sea and Desire present I did not hesitate. Without a thought of the combers I drove straight on, willing to meet instant death rather than to be shamed before them.

It turned out to be both easy and exciting. A great sea lifted us high and, crashing down with a deafening roar, carried us swiftly along on light foam as soft as eiderdown. As we were swept across the reef the turtle's plastron shell protected me from the coral. Little Sea and Desire had no need for protection; they were as much at home in the surf as a pair of periwinkles.

Sitting on his turtle, with many flourishes and more lies, Benny told the people of Puka-Puka how I had bravely grasped my ferocious brute, and how I had insisted on bringing in the male one, only he would not allow it. He added many marvelous details, in the true native fashion, for unless it is bragging about themselves, there is nothing in which Puka-Pukans

delight more than in telling of the prowess of their friends.

It is the law of the island that turtle and sail-fish belong to the entire population; so, if a man catches either of these creatures it is delivered to the head men of the villages and divided equally among all the population. When only one turtle is caught and shared among five hundred and fifty-odd inhabitants, the in-

dividual portions, one might think, would be small. But they are larger than the uninitiated would suspect, for of an average green turtle's three hundred pounds not ten are wasted. The Puka-Pukans eat the entire shell, the flippers, head, and tail. They consider the carapace and plastron shells the most delicate parts, so, when the turtle has been eaten, there is hardly enough refuse to fill a hat. On other islands half the turtle is thrown away, and I remember Viggo saying that although a turtle is a huge creature, there is very little meat on him.

The meat is red and tastes, to me, like a cross between beef and crab meat. The fat is green and is good for soup stock. In the female turtle are thousands and thousands of eggs, minute clusters, many of them no larger than pinheads, which will not hatch for ten, twenty, perhaps a hundred years! I believe I have seen as many as twenty thousand eggs in a single female, and I should not have been surprised to learn that there were twice that number. As a female lays only from four to five hundred eggs a year, one can easily calculate how long it will be before the smallest eggs are laid: fifty years, perhaps. Think of a pregnancy of fifty years! There are dozens of these clusters of a hundred or more minute eggs, and from that they range upward to fully developed ones the size of a hen's egg. The smaller eggs are a rare delicacy, but with me half the pleasure of eating them is lost because of the thought of the thousands of embryo lives I am destroying through the murderous grind of my molars.

Eight turtles were caught that day, only one of them by the people of Ura's village. The chief of police was mortified beyond words. He returned to his splendid coral-lime house, wrapped his head in a bundle of dirty rags, pleaded sick, and refused to be seen for three days. But on the fourth day he emerged, resplendent in blue trousers and red silk shirt, and, summoning his policemen, held a grand session of court to fine the villagers for straying pigs. All the pigs on Puka-Puka stray all the time, and as every one owns pigs Ura had no difficulty in choosing his victims. Thus, Leeward Village, which had shamed him by catching more turtles than his own settlement, was summoned *en masse* and each man fined a shilling. So Ura's dignity was reëstablished. But the fines were a small matter, for at Puka-Puka no one ever pays them.

While speaking of turtle-hunting, I will describe a much commoner way of catching the giant Chelonia.

I had been seriously ill from ptomaine-poisoning and decided to take a two weeks' vacation on Frigate Bird Islet. It is contrary to the local taboo for any one to visit Ko (or Frigate Bird) except during the copra-making seasons, when the entire population moves to the various islets; but as I was a foreigner and had been very *hapikipiki,* the fathers of Leeward Village generously permitted me to go to their islet. Furthermore, it was November, the season when the turtles come ashore to lay their eggs, and I had agreed to lie in wait for one.

Taking old William and Benny with me, I was soon camped in a little hut on the west point of Frigate Bird, in a grove of tall puka-trees where the wind moans with a pleasing dolorousness and a dozen species of sea-birds squawk discordantly from their perches in the branches. It is also a favorite nesting-place of the island doves (*rupe*), birds about the size of a bantam hen. Their cooing is in pleasing contrast to the sounds made by the other birds—a music as lonely sounding as the moaning of the wind through the puka-trees.

We had not been half an hour on Frigate Bird before William rushed back, his hat-brim askew, his arms flapping wildly. He had found a turtle's track only a short distance from the hut. It must have been a huge turtle, for its path was a good three feet wide.

When I had seen the furrow she had left behind her, I wondered that there is a turtle left alive in the sea; for the natives of all the islands know that the female lays her eggs every ten or twelve days four or five times during the months of November and December. When a track is found they have only to keep watch at the place during the tenth, eleventh, or twelfth night thereafter, at high tide, and they will catch the turtle when she returns to lay another batch of eggs. Each batch is laid within a hundred yards or so of the preceding one.

I remember reading somewhere that a turtle is very clever in hiding the spot where she lays her eggs, but this is nonsense. From the shallows to the shore brush she leaves a track as plain as an armored tank's, and the place where she deposits the eggs is hollowed out much like a hog-wallow, the sand being heaped a foot or more high over the eggs. After laying, she wobbles straight back to the reef, leaving another trail so deep and plain that one might stumble in it if one had failed to see it.

I have also read that she returns when the eggs hatch and eats many of her young. I have never observed or heard of such a thing on Puka-Puka. Here the eggs usually hatch in the daytime, and a green or a tortoise-shell turtle is never known to come ashore in the daytime, although occasionally they come at three or four in the morning, not returning until daybreak. When the eggs hatch, the first baby turtle digs a round hole to the surface and wobbles clumsily out, followed by a second, and a third, and so on, in single file. On reaching the surface they follow in single file to the shallows and dive in. Then the tragedy begins, for there is no morsel daintier than a baby turtle, and every fish seems to be waiting for them. Of the hundred that leave the beach, not more than fifty reach the reef, and in crossing it eight or ten more are gobbled up by spotted eels. Then, as soon as they are through the breakers, the big fish beyond swirl into them and swallow them to the last turtle.

How a baby turtle manages to escape its enemies during the first few months of life is a mystery to me. I have seen them hatch only once, and on that occasion, I am sure, not a turtle survived. The Puka-Pukans say that often all of them are eaten before they reach the reef. But a turtle lives for hundreds of years, and each year the female lays from four to six hundred eggs, so that in the two hundred and fifty thousand eggs she will lay in five hundred years a few young turtles escape to carry on the species.

William and Benny and I dug out one hundred and six round white eggs that day. They were not particularly palatable but quite good enough for three hungry men on Frigate Bird Islet. Benny decided that they had been laid two days before, so that we might expect Mrs. Turtle to return eight days later. Then we would lie in wait and catch her by turning her over on her back. Afterward we would make four signal fires on the north side of the islet, which, according to the code, would inform the villagers on the main islet that a turtle had been caught.

The eight days passed as I should like the rest of my life to pass. I paddled about in the lagoon with my water goggles on, slept in the shade on the beach, or sat on a coral mushroom fishing. Each day I grew stronger until I arrived at the stage of health when one derives the keenest delight from the mere fact of being alive.

On the eighth night we walked the beach during high tide, but when it had ebbed we returned to our little hut in the puka-grove and went to sleep. Benny explained that turtles seldom crossed the reef at low tide, but that this was not an absolute rule.

An hour later I awoke as completely refreshed as though I had enjoyed a long and dreamless night's sleep. William and Benny were snoring at the other end of the hut, and an owlish shearwater squawked a discordant love song to the moon, now an hour or more past the meridian.

I arose and crept out of the mosquito-net, thinking that Mrs. Turtle might have come ashore despite the low tide. Turning down the beach, I had not walked a hundred yards before I came to a fresh track plowed from the shallows to the shore brush. I stopped abruptly, for a moment unable to believe that this strange reptile from the mysterious sea had come ashore and was now actually in the brush only a few yards away. But on such a night anything seemed possible—anything but the commonplace.

The first ripples of the incoming tide were lapping over the reef and now a few inches of water lay over the coral between the reef and the shore. The water lay steely calm half-way out and the shadows of the coral stood forth with beautiful clearness. A tiny wall of water not more than a foot high swept shoreward, jet black save for the flashing flecks of spray that rose and subsided as the water rippled over the shallows. The patch of calm water dwindled until the wave broke with a faint hiss on the beach. A moment later the backwash was on its way out to the reef and soon the shallows were calm again, though now a few inches deeper than before.

Sitting in the sand near Mrs. Turtle's track, I peered into the shadows of the shore brush. Once I thought I saw her moving, but it was only the foliage stirred by the breeze. Several times I heard the crackle of breaking twigs as she broke through the brush.

She was quiet for a few moments, and then I heard

a sharp scraping noise, followed by the patter of sand against the brush foliage. I rose, crept close, and turned my flashlight in that direction. At my feet, so close that I could have touched her, was a huge green turtle, weighing at least three hundred pounds. She turned her head to stare at me with cold fishy eyes and then, with a deliberate, almost haughty motion, turned again to her work without paying me the least further attention.

Moving behind her, I sat down and placed my flashlight on the ground so that the light was fully on her. I expected her to move away, but she did not, and the natives have since told me that when a turtle has once started to dig the pit for her eggs, nothing can frighten her away. They say that her eggs must fall and she will go on with her work until her task is accomplished.

There was something solemn, almost religious, about that midnight labor, beset with danger, to prepare a nest for her young. I watched with a feeling akin to awe, as though eavesdropping on some esoteric rite. Did she know that death awaited her only a few feet away—that she would never cross the reef again to plunge into the cool sanctuary of the sea? If there was any terror in her reptilian brain she failed to show it. More likely she was the stoic she appeared to be, an inveterate fatalist whose hundreds of years of experience had placed her above the vicissitudes of life, or even of death itself. This light now turned upon her was merely another of those inexplicable phenomena which happen on that strange place, dry land. As I watched her I turned over all sorts of queer thoughts such as will come into a man's mind in the wee hours of a moonlight night on the remote beach of an uninhabited islet.

She dug her pit with her hind flippers, using the right and the left one alternately. With one flipper she would reach to a spot directly under her tail, scrape away about a handful of sand and gravel, and, cupping the bottom of her flipper, bring the sand to the surface and deposit it near the pit. Immediately the other flipper would be swung into the hole, while with the first she would brush away the sand she had brought to the surface. This was done by scraping the flipper vigorously across the ground, and it was that sound I had heard before coming up to her.

It was interesting to observe that, although one flipper was shorter than the other, when the hole became too deep for her to reach bottom with the short one, she still went through all the motions of scraping, cupping the flipper, and brushing the ground where the sand would have been. This somewhat lessened my opinion of Mrs. Turtle's common sense.

When the pit was as deep as she could make it—about twenty inches—she dropped in her eggs (one hundred and fourteen, as it later proved), filling the pit to within three or four inches of the surface. Then, working both her hind flippers at once, she scraped sand into the pit, patting it down firmly and pushing it under her plastron shell until she had a mound over the eggs about a foot high. Then for the first time she put her great powerful front flippers to work. Reaching out, she scraped them across the ground so vigorously that a shower of twigs and gravel went flying into the air. This was done, I suppose, to conceal the spot where she had laid her eggs, an entirely futile attempt. Half the shower was rained upon me with such force that I jumped to my feet. Deciding that I had seen enough of Mrs. Turtle's private affairs, I moved a few yards away to sit on the beach near her track. For ten minutes longer I heard her flinging the sand about; then she was silent.

I must have waited a full hour longer, for the moon had dropped close to Arai Reef, and I could see the foam and spray where the combers broke over the sunken coral. Venus had risen and in another hour dawn would break behind the puka-trees. I flashed my light twice into the brush, only to see Mrs. Turtle lying still, resting after her labor. Presently my head sank on my chest, and I dozed off for a few minutes.

I was aroused by a peculiar noise. It ceased the moment I looked up. There was Mrs. Turtle, perfectly still, not more than ten feet from me. I was directly in her path; all that I had to do was to walk up to her, get a firm grip on her carapace shell above the tail, and turn her over—but there was plenty of time for that.

I watched her for fully ten minutes; then all at once she breathed. It was a raucous respiration, sounding startlingly loud in the still night air. Perhaps it was the long exposure under the moon's full light that made me act as I did. At any rate, it occurred to me that Mrs. Turtle was an exceedingly human sort of creature, so I decided to have a little confidential chat with her.

I explained the great mistake she had made in coming to a populous island to lay her eggs. "In your hundreds of years," I said, "you should have learned that only the loneliest sandbanks are safe for you, and that your greatest danger is from an encounter with man.

"And now, madam," I went on with a little flourish, "see what your lack of forethought has brought you to. To-morrow you will be split in two—*Vavaji ake,* as the Puka-Pukans say—and eaten to the last corner of your shell. You will have ceased to exist. For many hundreds of years you have flopped across the reefs of lonely atolls, plowed up the beaches, and laid your hundred eggs; for centuries you have paddled with dignified deliberation about the seven seas, dining on the choicest turtle grass, and contemplating the starry firmament through long tropic nights. All these centuries you have escaped being made into soup for aldermen's dinners; you have escaped the spears and ropes of savages; and, most amazing of all, at about the time William the Conqueror crossed the English Channel, when you hatched out on some remote and moonlit tropic beach, you escaped your enemies in the sea and by some freak of chance managed to grow to maturity, safe from all sea creatures, only now to be unceremoniously flopped over by a mere South Sea trader.

"Outside the reef old Papa Turtle is waiting for

you. When he rises to breathe he gazes shoreward, wondering what is keeping you so late. But he shall never see you again. He will wait beyond the reef for a few days, and then, perhaps, he will paddle off in search of another mate. To-morrow your body, from the tip of your nose to the end of your tail, will be ground between the jaws of five hundred hungry savages. What a forlorn end to a life of adventure such as yours!"

Again Mrs. Turtle breathed hoarsely, and this time she struck her flipper on the sand with a loud slap as though annoyed that I should keep her waiting. I rose and stepping behind her grasped her shell. I made a feeble attempt to turn her over, but as she was very heavy I did not try again, for I was willing to believe that she was too heavy for me. She waddled slowly down the beach, while I stood where I was, watching her. When she had almost reached the water I cried, "And now, madam, I will give you three pieces of advice: Drive deeply and at once whenever you see a ship, boat, or canoe. Never go ashore at an island where you see fires at night. And above all, avoid man, your greatest enemy."

Old Mrs. Turtle wobbled on without so much as a glance back, flopped gracelessly into the water, and disappeared. Dawn was at hand as I walked back to the puka-grove; Benny and old William were still asleep.

Neither of them would speak respectfully to me all that day. They soon discovered the turtle tracks and my own as well. They knew what had happened, but they were unable to account for my strange behavior. And when we returned to the main islet the following day and people heard the story, I was in disgrace. William cursed horribly in four languages, and Benny emitted such a splutter of "ifs" that he nearly choked in the process. For all that, I am glad I acted as I did; and if Mrs. Turtle is capable of emotion, I am sure that she is glad too.

VIII

A Debate at Leeward Village

Ke kave 'u i toku panga
Ka moe tau'a i te ware o te matua,
Taua i toku yana wawine;
Ki akuiroa i te wui tane
E wawine koe noo kiaku.

I shall sleep on a mat of pandanus
Before the house of her father,
I and my chosen woman
Will thus betroth one another.

—*From* "Mako Ono-ono" (*a Puka-Puka love song*).

VIII

A Debate at Leeward Village

LITTLE SEA and Desire sat outside my cook-house while I prepared supper. I would not allow them to come in, for I wanted to surprise them with a European meal. I made a soup and fried some croutons; then I fried some chicken Maryland style. Entrées were string beans and taro *au gratin*. There was also a fine salad made from a coconut-tree bud Benny had brought, a tin of pine-apple cubes and a saucer of condensed milk and Benedictine for dessert, with coffee and tinned cheese to wind up with. To wash all this down I mixed a Janusfaced rum punch which tasted like lemonade but encouraged conversation. The table was set with my best gilt-edged china, knives, forks, and all the other furnishings of the civilized dinner-table. When all was ready I sent my assistant, Benny, about his business and asked the two sea nymphs to join me.

They had neglected to dress for the occasion, and

came in grass skirts and nothing else. Mistaking my soup for a curious kind of sauce, they mashed the taro and beans in it and ate the mess with their fingers. The knives and forks were used to beat dance rhythms on the table.

After a round of punch, Little Sea and her cousin began to chatter like a flock of mynah birds. I followed them in matters of etiquette and we had a jolly time of it.

While dallying over our coffee and cheese—Desire used the cheese to putty cracks in the table—Little Sea told me that the men of Leeward Village were going to meet that night to discuss the matter of King-of-the-Sky's wife, who claimed that she had not received as large a share of the turtle as her neighbor enemy, Mrs. George. The discussion was to take place at the village meeting-house in the interior of the islet, where nobody would disturb them.

We agreed to eavesdrop at the meeting, and after a final round of punch we blew out the light, sneaked through the village, and followed a path into the coconut-groves.

The night was pitch black. I could barely distinguish Little Sea moving before me like a shadow on a black curtain. Often I stumbled off the trail altogether, when Desire, who was behind, would catch me by the *pareu* tail and pull me back on the path with some disparaging remark about cowboys who can't see in the dark.

Before long a rumbling sound reached our ears: it was the first low mutterings of the discussion which was soon to echo through the groves from the lagoon beach to the outer reef.

The meeting-house was built on a knoll made by the ancients, who had banked up the sand in excavating their taro-beds, and was nothing but a thatch roof supported by a dozen six-foot poles. Within sat the fathers of Leeward Village, all of them talking at once, no one listening to the others, and, as is the case the world over, each disputant glorying in the belief that his cogent arguments were being heard.

King-of-the-Sky, whose wife had been so shabbily treated in the turtle division by not being given more than her due share, sat with his great back to one of the house posts. He roared intermittently, sweeping his paws in comprehensive gestures; and at such times I thought that the others were silenced, but by the dim shell fire burning near-by I could see that their mouths were still working: it was only that King-of-the-Sky's roarings had deafened my ears to the others.

It was a glorious debate. Thus would King-of-the-Sky present his wife's complaint, holding strictly to the matter in question:

"Liars! Thieves! Who are you to dare speak to me? Who am I to stand your insults? I am King-of-the-Sky, son of the great canoe-builder Hog-Tooth, grandson of the marvelous fisherman Nose, and a descendant of the superman Great Stomach, who caught turtles by flying over the reef and picking them up by their tails! Who am I? I am King-of-the-Sky, the greatest man on Puka-Puka!"

Here the air reverberated as he struck his barrel-like chest.

"I am King-of-the-Sky, the strongest man on Puka-Puka, the strongest man in all the Cook Islands! Didn't I sail my great canoe, the largest in the world, four days out to sea with the wife of Sore-Nose? Didn't I catch the shark that it required four men to pull in? Haven't the women of Puka-Puka been ravished by me?" Again he struck his chest a resounding blow.

Up jumped a sawed-off little man, screaming in a high-pitched voice and never once mentioning the turtle, merely relating the exploits of his ancestors and telling what a redoubtable man he himself was. Then the discussion again became general—a general pandemonium—until King-of-the-Sky bellowed out again, when all other voices were drowned in his lion's roar.

Little Sea had edged comfortably close to me. "*Aué!*" she said. "King-of-the-Sky will win as he always does. He isn't even hoarse yet."

"Are the debates won by the man who makes the most noise?" I asked.

"Of course! How else should they be won?" she asked quite seriously. "Isn't that the way it is in your country?"

I was reminded of a Democratic national convention I had once heard from a distance of six blocks, and I was forced to admit that it was even the same in the white man's land.

One by one the Leeward Villagers left the meeting

until, at midnight, only King-of-the-Sky and half a dozen other lusty-throated ones were left. Soon after we too returned to the village, whereupon Desire went into the hut, while Little Sea and I sat on a coconut frond that lay invitingly before the door. Then—I don't know exactly how it happened, but it seemed the only thing to do under the circumstances, and I could think of no reason for not doing it; furthermore, I felt that our happiness depended upon it. So I lay down and fell asleep with Little Sea's head resting on my arm.

Some time afterward I was aroused by the sound of voices. They belonged to Mr. Chair and his brotherhood, returning from a midnight assembly on the outer beach. Mr. Chair saw the two dim objects lying before the door.

"That's why Mr. Cigarette was absent to-night!" I heard him say. "It's against the rules, for Little Sea has not been initiated!"

"Oh, well, never mind," said Mr. Horse. "He's a cowboy and isn't supposed to understand the customs of Puka-Puka."

Then I heard Miss Button say, snappishly: "Who cares? The little hussy! What does she amount to? As for that person Ropati-Cowboy, I didn't like him anyway. There are plenty of other fish in the sea."

The society then disappeared and vanished in the shadows.

I awoke about four. Little Sea was still fast asleep. She was mine now, I reflected, for it is an old Puka-Puka custom that a man shall publicly proclaim a woman as his mate by sleeping at her side before the door of her father's house.

I turned to Little Sea and kissed her cheek.

There was a rumbling sound from somewhere in the depths of the islet. King-of-the-Sky was sitting alone in the Leeward Village meeting-house, gesticulating to the attentive shades of night, roaring out the genealogy of his ancestors, telling the sleeping world of his greatness.

IX

Puka-Puka Religion—Old Style

Ka piri taua ki te po-mata,
Waka uri ki te varua toa,
Waka tere taku vaka kia Maroroji—
Wenua mamao no te toa Taua.

Close to the sky-eyes of the night,
Dancing with the souls of dead warriors,
You shall sail away in the canoe of the Sky-God—
In Taua's canoe, to the home of the trade-wind.

—*From* "Mako Mate" (*chant of the dead*).

Puka-Puka Religion—Old Style

WHEN a primitive man dances to rouse the love-impulse in his chosen woman, he is keenly aware of the purpose of his dance; and when Puka-Pukans chant their long romantic songs for the dead, they believe that the song's description of a blissful state for departed spirits is actually evoking such a state. A Puka-Puka woman chants over the dead body of her husband:

> Close to the sky-eyes of the night,
> Dancing with the souls of dead warriors,
> You shall sail away in the canoe of the Sky-God—
> In Taua's canoe, to the home of the trade-wind.

And even at the present day she still believes that without these chants—and dances, too, for they are accompanied by a rhythmic motion of body and arms—the dead man's soul would meet with but a poor reception in the hereafter. The efficacy of these chants, with their imaginative descriptions of a future life, is so implicitly believed in that even the missionaries have failed to relegate them to the rubbish heap where most Polynesian traditions and beliefs have long since lain buried and forgotten.

I have seen many Puka-Puka dances. The memory of two of them in particular remains vividly in my mind.

One clear moonless night I left my veranda to walk along the lagoon beach. Passing Central Village, I came to a deep bay a quarter of a mile in width. The water lay cool and beguiling before me, sparkling with the dancing reflections of the stars—the "sky-eyes of the night" as my neighbors call them. Without having any particular destination in mind, I girdled up my *pareu,* waded into the bay, and swam in leisurely fashion to the opposite shore. I could see the coconut-shell fires flaring in the village behind and the phosphorescent water in my wake glowing with pale light. Upon reaching the sandy beach I heard from the groves ahead a rhythmic clapping of hands and followed in the direction of the sound.

Soon I came upon four people in a little glade in the midst of a curious rite. One old woman tended a fire; two other grandams sat facing one another, clapping their hands, and in the space between was a little girl, not more than five years old, dancing. She was being taught the erotic dances of the women so that when she herself should grow to womanhood she might be desirable in men's eyes.

It was a deeply serious ritual. The old women's faces were impassive as they leaned forward, their bodies swaying slightly, regarding the baby with fascinated eyes, and muttering a song so old that it is doubtful if even they understood the sense of it. The little girl danced tirelessly, gravely. Her tiny hands would fly to her hips as she wriggled through a movement that would have been sensuous for a woman but was only pretty for her. Then her hands would join daintily over her head, and while gazing at some imagined lover in the overhanging darkness, she would go through, step by step, the movements performed by the older women on the great fête days. Now and then one of the crones would rise stiffly and perform, as well as her old bones would permit, some complicated movement, while her three ancient companions clapped their hands, nodding their heads in approbation.

Here, I thought, is something far more ancient than the church lore so assiduously crammed down my neighbor's throats—a ritual as important, as full of meaning as the dance of the warriors who celebrate a victory before the battle is fought. I remembered my own childhood when everything had been thus acted in the imagination before it had been experienced in reality. In civilized countries little girls play at being mothers, and little boys at being soldiers, and when left to themselves they are quite as serious as the little island girl who was playing at love. But the little Puka-Pukan girl, despite her babyhood, must have been vaguely aware that she was being instructed in a magical ceremony whose purpose was to gain her a fine husband when she grew older. No doubt she had been told, and believed, that by playing at love she would eventually obtain love.

II

I saw another and more spectacular dance one night some months later when Benny persuaded me to leave my books and go with him for a stroll.

He led me to a moonlit glade where we lay on a knoll under the pandanus-trees. Before us was the glittering coral sand leading down to the sea, where land-crabs were scuttling about at the water's edge. The odor of roasting fish rose on the wind as it hummed softly through the palm tops; the sea thundered on the reef, and inland, among the trees, I could see the vague silhouettes of thatched houses where the old people, afraid of the spirits, crouched around tiny fires.

Across the glade, clearly outlined against the sky, was a naked boy perched on the limb of a dead tree, high above the ground. He was as silent as a sphinx, and looked scarcely human as he sat there with a first-quarter moon shining over his shoulder. Once he stood erect, yawned, stretched himself, looked about, and then resumed his squatting position.

Under the trees by the beach was a grass hut open on the landward side. In front of it flared a fire of coconut shells where two old men were roasting fish.

They too were squatting, their heads between their knees, their grotesque shadows blotting out the little hut behind them.

Suddenly the silence of the groves was shattered by the shrill cry of a boy who came leaping through the glade waving a flambeau and yelling that the old women were coming—coming to dance in the moonlight.

Presently here they came and formed in a double line down the glade, dancing to a rhythm beaten out by three old men. Some were lean and some were fat; two of the youngest of them held babies in their arms; late-born babies of gray-haired mothers. Bones rattled

and heads bobbed as they danced their witches' rigadoon—grinning ancient sirens with toothless gums and limp-skinned faces, fat old grandams unsteady on their feet, and dear old Mama leading them! There was a flower behind her withered ear and rags of lace hung from her mildewed bedgown. She shrieked the orders of the dance in a ducking-stool tone as she wriggled in sensuous movements, barren of significance, and frantically waved her long, emaciated arms. Children played in and out of the line, screaming an accompaniment to the old dames' cackle and sometimes imitating the dance. The boy in the dead tree gazed owlishly down from his perch before the moon. One of the old men in front of the grass hut let his fish burn on the coals as he watched the dancers, thinking, doubtless, of the time when they were firm-breasted virgins and he a supple-limbed youth. He turned to grin at the other old man, and then mumbled peevishly as he raked his scorched fish out of the coals.

"My grandmother dances well," Benny said, pointing to an old lady at the end of the line. I thought her far less skilful than the others, so I said nothing. She could not follow the movements of the dance; she was always a measure or two behind the others. When their arms shot out, hers remained at her side or rocked at her breast in a cradling motion. When other fleshless hips gyrated, she did a tottering *pas seul* of her own. She gazed at the moon, smiling weirdly, unconscious of the fact that she was behindhand in all of her movements. Her dress hung in rags to her feet, and there was a withered flower stuck jauntily in hair damp with fish-oil.

One hideous old crone chanced to see Benny and me watching the dance from the shadows. She came hopping toward us with the self-confidence of youth, for, perhaps, in the magic of the dance she thought herself young and beautiful again. Before we were aware of her intention she pressed a kiss on each of our cheeks. Her lips were clammy, but in her rheumy eyes there still burned the light of vague desire.

One by one the old women, exhausted by their unaccustomed exertions, withdrew into the shadows of the groves, and at last only Benny's grandmother was left, dancing on, not aware that she was alone. Still she gazed at the moon with the same weird smile on her lips, while she tottered through the movements of the dance, rocking her body in a vaguely remembered way. It was an éerie sight to see, her withered form etched against the moonlit sky.

Of a sudden she stopped to look about her. A deep hush had fallen over everything. The naked boy in the tree slipped from his perch and vanished. The old men's fire was dead now and the thatched huts in the groves had crumbled into the darkness. A harsh wind seemed to blow through the old woman's bones, the solitude seemed to frighten her. Whimpering plaintively, she hobbled off into the groves to find her old companions.

That, too, was a ritualistic dance, the only one of its kind I have ever seen, but undoubtedly it was common enough in the old days. It was the same form of magic practised by the little girl, but she had been looking forward to life, while these old women were thinking of death, moving their withered limbs through the erotic movements of the dance of love as they hope to do again in the world of ghosts when they have left their worn-out bodies behind them and are

> Close to the sky-eyes of the night,
> Dancing with the souls of dead warriors.

X

Puka-Puka Religion—New Style

Taku ove tangi t'eao,
Yolo te kakai p'u ki Tiona.
Akahuru 'u toku pirip'u,
Na mumura pe te mata o te ra,
Ta ke motia te tamawine
I toku y'elenga ki Tiona:
Ukaina taua e toku yana wawine.

The church bell rings in the morning;
Men, suitably dressed, all go to Zion;
I draw on my trousers,
They are red like the eye of the sun.
They dazzle the young maidens
As I pass on to Zion.
I greet you, my gift-woman.

—*From a modern Puka-Puka chant,* "Waiva Tangata."

Puka-Puka Religion—New Style

THE Puka-Pukans call their church "Zion." Every Sunday morning Husks beats the tom-toms to announce the service, whereupon all the inhabitants don their most highly prized finery and throng forth Zionward—all of them excepting old William, the heathen. One by one they pass my trading-station and turn into the churchyard, only a few steps beyond. It is a bizarre sight. If such costumes were to be seen in an American town one would think that a crowd of lunatics had escaped from the state asylum.

King-of-the-Sky is usually the first to appear, dressed in a swallow-tail coat and tight trousers made of cloth of a vivid green. The coat is double-breasted, with two rows of large brass buttons, eight to a row. Beneath it appears the mighty hairy chest of King-of-the-Sky, for what cares he for such trifles as shirts, collars, or neckties?

Scratch-Woman (Raku-raku-wawine) appears, wearing a black lace dress which was probably discard-

ed by the wife of some trading skipper, thrown overboard, perhaps, close to Puka-Puka reef, and salvaged by some ancestor of Scratch-Woman, to be forever treasured by his descendants. She also wears a pair of men's striped socks, and her huge feet are squeezed into a pair of ancient high-heeled shoes. She approaches Zion lifting her feet high at every step, as though she were walking over logs, and sets them carefully down, having learned by experience that gravelly ground makes precarious footing on Sundays.

George, grandson of Ura, wears a heavy British army overcoat and a bowler hat set at a rakish angle. His feet are shod in brogues that would do credit to a colored minstrel. Now and then he draws a yard-square turkey-red handkerchief from his pocket to mop his brow; but sympathy would be wasted on

George. What is a little discomfort to a man convinced that he is the best-dressed individual on Puka-Puka?

Ears has somehow assembled an almost complete golfer's costume. He has checked knickerbockers, striped woolen stockings, a golfer's cap, but alas! no brogues. Therefore he must walk to church in his stocking feet, and many such journeys have, of course, told sadly on the stockings. His huge toes and calloused heels are indecently displayed among ragged shreds of yarn.

Dear old Mama never fails to wear her ancient bedgown, from which hang shreds of lace sewn there, perhaps, by some bride of the eighteen-nineties. On her head she wears the crown of William's straw hat. True lovers they must have been, years ago, when

William acquired the hat, giving her the crown while only the brim was reserved for himself.

Ura, chief of police and deacon of the church, comes in a commodore's coat, decorated with epaulets and an abundance of tarnished brass braid. It had been a present from one of Her Britannic Majesty's ships which visited Puka-Puka forty years ago.

So it goes. The Puka-Puka church parade is the most heterogeneous display of rags and tags that may be seen anywhere outside of Bedlam. Once when Table Winning was viewing it with me—having come to Puka-Puka with Viggo for a two days' visit—he said: "What a mess the missionaries have made of it with their eternal harping on clothing the disgusting body, covering it from head to toes lest some carnally minded person see this obscene envelop of flesh the Lord God gave each of us! Here we see the result: they have only succeeded in organizing a weekly, Sabbath-day procession of scarecrows and buffoons!" And that's about the truth of the matter.

II

Sometimes I myself go to Zion, having nothing better to do. I wait until Sea Foam the preacher walks pompously past wearing his bandmaster hat and his celluloid collar; then I shin down a veranda post and follow him into the church.

The service is much as it is at home: there are prayers, hymns, and a sermon, but here the hymns are sung with Polynesian gusto, interlarded with grunts from the young fry and piercing countermelodies sung *à solo* by one or another of the village virtuosos. Many hymns are sung, and at last Sea Foam clears his voice, steps forward, and begins:

"Members of this church of Zion, young men, old men, deacons, Christians—health to us! This is the word of God as it is written on the Taboo Book: it says that the birth of Jesus was like this: When Mary was betrothed to Joseph he did not know that she was with child; but later Mary told him of this. Of course Joseph, being only a foolish white man, was very angry and called her many bad names; but the angel of God appeared to him and said that Mary had spoken the truth when she said that she was with child and still a virgin. This child, the angel said, would be a Son of God and would bring the church to the children of these islands and also to the white men.

"God was right when he gave His child to a virgin to bear, for do you think that a hard woman (*wawine maro*) like you women here could have borne him? Of course, we children of the islands do not understand how such a thing could happen; but it is so written in the Taboo Book, and therefore it is the truth."

Sea Foam rumbles and rambles on, filling an hour with his profound theological speculations. When he comes to the prayer, he sometimes does me the honor of personally recommending me to the Lord, advising him that I am a worthy man and begging him to condone my occasional peccadillos.

My interest frequently wanes before he has reached the end of his sermon and I lean back staring at the great thatched roof. It must contain at least ten thousand square feet of pandanus-leaf thatch, each sheaf being laid with mathematical precision and bound to coconut-wood plaiting with fine native sennit. The various supports, rafters, braces, and plates are of pandanus logs of a rich oily brown, and make one think of a sylvan cathedral where hamadryads might very well dance, where Syrinx might be chased by Pan, Daphne by Apollo, and various other heathen rites take place in the dark hours before the dawn.

The service is often disturbed by some one chopping wood just beyond the churchyard. When we come forth we are all horrified, as usual, to find that it is old William, the heathen, who, after sleeping the whole week, has wakened just in time to chop wood of a Sunday morning, thereby expressing his contempt for religion and religious people. To wheedle myself back into his favor and also as a token of my respect for his courage, I invite him into the store and refresh him with a mighty goblet of rum.

XI

The Death of the Sandpiper

Wakapoteka au i toku tuki-wenua
Ki te ak'u, tuki ki te turi—
Aue ma toku yana wawine.

I roll my cannon to the sea reef,
Bang! I kill the sandpiper—
The maidens cheer my sharpshooting.

—*From* "Mako Tuki Manu" (*Puka-Puka huntsman's chant.*)

XI
The Death of the Sandpiper

I SOMETIMES think that I have lived at Puka-Puka long enough to know something of my neighbors' mental processes, to understand them individually and collectively. Some grave old grandmother or grandfather will stop at the store to pass the time of day with me, or I will see the village fathers deliberating in one of their monthly assemblies, and they appear to be very much like parents and grandparents at home. Then something will happen to convince me that these men and women of mature stature are, have been, and always will be children, and in order to account for their actions I have to hark back to my own childhood days. Thus it was in the affair of the sandpiper.

One day, walking along the causeway leading from Leeward to Central Village, I encountered my friend, old William, the lone infidel of Danger Island, and stopped to have a yarn with him. It was a Monday morning, and, as I had been to church the previous day, I had again to make my peace with William, who looked upon my occasional back-slidings with ill-disguised contempt.

"Puka-Puka men all damn fool Christians! Bloody lubbers!" he said. "Whas a matter, you? Whas a matter you go to church for?"

"Well, William, it's this way," I said. "Little Sea belongs to the church, and now that she is living with me, I go now and then to please her."

"Hmm!" grunted William. He took off his hat brim to scratch his head, swatted a bloated mosquito that had been dining on one of his great ears, and then went on irrelevantly, "Puka-Puka damn fine island. Plenty eat, plenty sleep, no work—not like when I was a boy on whaling ship."

This profound reflection seemed to have exhausted him and he said no more for a time. Of a sudden he cocked his head to one side in a listening attitude. Then, to my great astonishment, he opened his great white-fanged mouth and chirped, *"Twit-twit! Twit-twit!"* in a high ridiculous voice not at all like his ordinary speaking voice. A moment later he jumped up and went hobbling off at a great rate, chirping his plaintive *"twit-twit! twit-twit!"* and disappeared in the brush.

I observed then that Puka-Puka had unaccountably roused itself from its usual mid-morning stupor. One old man, so decrepit that I had thought he could never again leave his hut, came charging down the causeway with the rest of the inhabitants close behind him, all of them chirping *"twit-twit! twit-twit!"* like a parcel of lunatics. King-of-the-Sky passed, carrying the village shotgun. He is a huge man, six feet four on bare hoofs and composed of two hundred and seventy pounds of solid bone and muscle. Every one was greatly excited and all hurried in one direction and scattered through the trees and bush inland.

For a moment I was too greatly astonished to move; then an infectious madness seized me. I did a caper on the narrow causeway, let out a whoop and a few "*twit-twits*" on my own account, and followed in the wake of the others.

I found them gathered about one of the taro excavations, partially hidden by bush and puka-trees. It had been raining and there were six or eight inches of water over the mud where the plants grew. Every one was "*twit-twitting,*" from the great-grandfathers to the babies who had only just learned to walk.

King-of-the-Sky stood in the middle of the taro-bed, waist-deep in mud and water. His six-inch mouth was spread even wider in a smile of great self-importance; he held his gun at the ready while his gaze followed the flutterings of a lone sandpiper that circled about the swamp.

With a flutter the sandpiper approached to within thirty feet of King-of-the-Sky. He raised his gun slowly; a terrific explosion followed, the rebound upsetting the superman into the mud. A cloud of smoke rose over the taro-beds, while the poor little sandpiper turned a dozen aërial somersaults and landed with a splash in the swamp. Thereupon King-of-the-Sky plunged through the muck and retrieved his prey, while the villagers shouted "*Mate! Mate!*" ("He is dead! He is dead!") Forthwith the crowd dispersed as quickly as it had assembled. Every one had rushed home to witness the second act in this, to me, still mysterious little atoll diversion.

Soon King-of-the-Sky appeared sauntering, mud-bespattered, through Leeward Village, the shotgun on his shoulder and the sandpiper swinging in his hand. A few of the children followed him, but all the older people were seated in front of their houses so that when he passed they could cry in the truly ingenuous native fashion:

"Where have you been, King-of-the-Sky?"

"*Aué!* Look! He's shot a sandpiper!"

All of them appeared to be enormously surprised, as though they had not themselves witnessed King-of-the-Sky's heroic adventure.

A few moments later, the little show at an end, the street was again deserted. Every one had moved into the shade of their houses to resume their disturbed siestas.

XII

Mataueа Point

Akara ki toku buka moana,
Koa yuayua, koa vero ake tu ko te ao.
"*Euriia maata, ka mate taua*
E toku yana wawine!
Nai te yala?
Nai makatia ki te tai
Na pukuna i te ika koa tere rararo?"
Toru po, toru ao,
Puaki Kinieve!

I look into the book of the sea,
The clouds are thick, the sun is hidden.
"A great hurricane comes; we shall die,
And my beautiful mistress!
Who is the sinner?
Whom shall we throw into the sea,
To the whale that swims neath the surface?"
Three days, three nights,
And he shall be vomited on Nineveh!

—*From* "Mako Moana" (*a Puka-Puka sea chant*).

XII

Matauea Point

EZEKIEL, my customer of the pound note and the talcum-powder, is the best canoe builder on the island, and I engaged him to make me a craft. It turned out to be a beautiful specimen of native workmanship. (At present it is in the Bishop Museum at Honolulu, for a few years ago I sold it to an anthropologist from that place.) The joints were lashed together with a specially prepared sennit and were so perfect that no calking or putty of any kind was used; nevertheless, it was thoroughly water-tight.

Each part of a Puka-Puka canoe, no matter if only a tiny piece of wood a few inches long, or the notch on the phallic symbol at the stern, has a name peculiar to the island. All the canoes are remarkably seaworthy; within the lives of some of the present generation, Puka-Puka canoes have safely reached Samoa, a distance of four hundred miles, and old legends are filled with references to journeys to Tahiti, Rarotonga, and other even more distant islands. One song legend tells of a journey to Rapa-Nui (Easter Island), a fact which should interest anthropologists.

Some five months after he had started work Ezekiel had my canoe finished—an unusual record, for Puka-Pukans usually spend years at such a task. The three villages were again repairing to their respective islets to gather coconuts, so I bundled Little Sea and her cousin Desire into my little vessel (with other necessary provisions for comfort) and sailed for Matauea Point. Sea Foam had given me the use of the mission's hut there, and I was soon settled for two of the most idyllic and exciting weeks of my life.

Matauea was formerly the stronghold of a powerful village headed by two supermen; but for many generations it has been deserted by all but their shades. Sea Foam makes occasional sojourns there, for he claims not to believe in the apparitions of men who have never read the Bible. According to the natives, these spirit forms are often seen, and they have so impressed on me the fact of their reality that I have many times imagined that I have seen them among the trees or floating like reef spray along the wide stretches of beach. Little Sea and Desire had many a fright while we were on the Point, but their fears were somewhat relieved by the thought that no Puka-Pukan ghost would dare approach a white man, more particularly if he happened to be a cowboy.

The Point overlooks the reef and cloud-mantled sea on one side, and on the other a horseshoe-shaped bay much like the one on the main islet, but larger. Here the bay is more than a mile across, mottled with

fragments of reef and coral mushrooms which divide water so deep that one can barely see the outlines of the coral bottom sixty feet below. The beach is of yellow and white sand, and coconut-palms and pandanus-trees grow to the water's edge, the spring tides even washing about their roots. At the head of the bay are the brown huts of the copra makers; at night great fires are built there, and while I sit on the beach with a ground line, I watch the play of firelight on the water until my attention is engaged by a red-snapper that has taken my bait.

All the sea foods common to these waters are found in great abundance near the Point, and many birds nest in the trees by the outer beach, though for some reason they avoid the rest of the islet. But the great attraction of the place is its cleanness: no mud, dirt, dust—only the clean white sand over which blows the full force of the trade-wind singing through the fronds of the palms with such regularity that, at the time of a lull, one stops to listen, feeling that something unaccountable has happened, not conscious at the moment that it is only that the wind has died away. But it is never for long: soon it makes up again, bringing refreshing coolness to the atoll dwellers.

For two weeks we lived there, fishing, eating, swimming, sleeping, playing, loving, with torchlight expeditions at night for coconut crabs and sea birds; with long swims across the bay from one coral head to another where we could rest and eat raw *paua* clams. Sometimes we did nothing at all, merely lying in the shade on the beach, sensuously enjoying the gifts of God.

One day Little Sea suggested that we go hunting. Taking my shotgun and a pocketful of cartridges, and with Desire skipping puppylike at our heels, we walked along the outer beach, scouting for sandpipers, for they were more abundant on Ko Islet than on Puka-Puka, where King-of-the-Sky had galvanized the inhabitants by shooting his one bird.

The trade-wind blew unceasingly, cooled and cleansed by its journey over thousands of miles of empty sea and scented by its passage through the tamanu-groves of Ko Islet. The wind and the scudding cloud patches cooled us as we crept from bush to bush, with eyes alert for the terrible sandpiper. Invariably one of the girls saw the birds first; long-legged, foolish-looking creatures, with patchwork feathers and a bill projection like an unsmoked cigar. They hopped about on the exposed lagoon coral near the beach, seeming to find any number of interesting things to fill their crops with.

I banged away, greatly to the girls' delight, and presently had a round dozen, four apiece, just enough. While I had been stalking the birds Little Sea had found some coconut crabs—vicious-clawed brutes like gigantic hermit crabs minus their shells. Their abdomens are full of a fatty meat with a delicious coconut flavor. It is the richest food I have ever eaten, and for this reason I soon learned to partake of it sparingly.

We reached a high bank of coral gravel half-way round the islet, where Desire joined us with her arms full of clams. Close by, in a pretty little glade, the girls set to work cleaning the birds. Then they lit a fire and threw on it some husked sprouted coconuts to cook. In these sprouted nuts the water has been absorbed, and in its place is a ball of pulpy white substance which fills the entire cavity. It is delicious, especially when cooked in the nuts, for then much of the oil from the surrounding meat is absorbed by the pulp, or *uto,* as it is called in the islands.

Our meal was soon ready, and never have I relished a meal more than that one. It was spread on green fronds that Desire had plaited into a mat. There were broiled sandpipers and shearwaters, coconut crabs, baked clams oozing a succulent sauce, *utos,* drinking nuts, coconut-bud salad, and set before me as a special delicacy was a long fat sea centipede that Desire had unearthed while digging clams.

We ate like true savages, tearing the birds to pieces with our fingers, crunching the smaller bones and gnawing the flesh from the larger ones with grunts of satisfaction. And when our faces were smeared with the savory broiled fat we licked our lips with rotary sweeps of the tongue. The sandpipers were as plump and tender as squab, and far more savory. Civilized cooks usually insist on spoiling the fine natural flavor of game by adding needless sauces, spices, and herbs, so that one tastes a very palpable sauce but must rely upon his eyes to inform him as to the nature of the meat. To me the finest way to cook a fowl is to broil it over odorless coals, salting it to taste, and basting it betimes with good sweet butter. Give me this, and you may have your Neuberg fricassee, sage-dressed, curried fowls. To my way of thinking they are lifeless foods, reminding one of stews that have been warmed over until all the vitalizing properties have been cooked out.

Having stuffed ourselves to repletion, we stowed the remaining food in frond baskets, stretched out under the trees, and went to sleep. Late in the afternoon we jumped into a pool by the outer reef for a swim and then returned to the Point. Desire skipped on ahead, Little Sea and I following in more leisurely fashion as befitted two lovers. Suddenly she stopped and grasped my arm. Then, with a laugh, she led me into the bush to a flat coral slab.

"Do you remember the night you gave me the dress?" she asked. "Well," I hid it until morning, when everybody was asleep; then I slipped it under my *pareu* and sneaked out here, just like a cowboy, dodging behind trees so that no one would see me. When I reached this spot I dug a hole and buried the dress, for I was afraid that people would see it and say that I was loving you for money."

While she told me this her pretty hands were busily scooping away the gravel. Presently she uncovered another slab, removed it, and there below was my muslin dress, none the better for a year of interment. She picked it up, saying that she would give it to Desire, but it broke into shreds in her hands.

We reached the Point just as a flood of sunset light was dripping from the heavens, staining the lagoon an ominous, sanguinary hue.

II

The next day the lagoon was lifeless, steely, reflecting each cloud and the littoral of the bay so clearly that, lying on the beach, I could easily imagine the real sky beneath and the reflection overhead. Toward noon curtain clouds formed high up, deepening gradually until the groves were almost as dark as night. On the reef great seas were pounding and countless sea birds circled about screaming plaintively.

Shortly before six the sun forced its way through the clouds, with its disk only a few degrees above the horizon. Instantly the whole cloud-dome was illuminated with a flaming red light, as bright to east as west. It was a sight to fill one with fear. The groves, the lagoon, the beach absorbed it until all other hues were lost in a blood-red effulgence that seemed to glow in the very air itself. When the sun went down, the light vanished by rapid perceptible degrees, and in a moment, it seemed, pitchy darkness had set in.

Still there was no wind. Crawling beneath the mosquito-net, we listened to the great seas bombarding the reef; they seemed intent on crumbling the tiny islet to powder and distributing it along the bottom of the Pacific. From time immemorial that insignificant crumb of land, with its banks of sand ostentatiously decorated with a few coconut-trees, had broken the serene march of the great rollers on their way across the Pacific; now the time had come for reparation. The mighty combers crashed down with long echoing reverberations like the roar of great cannon, followed by the ominous swish of broken water rushing across the reef in mad clouds of foam and spray.

As I listened it seemed to me that the islet had become very small, had shrunk to a mere sand-bank which was being ravenously devoured by twenty-foot combers. Between the roar of the breakers I could hear the sea-birds' dismal foreboding cries from the coconut-palms, and the incessant hum of countless mosquitoes outside the net.

I felt light-headed; grotesque hallucinations materialized before me with startling vividness. I was afraid and found myself edging closer to Little Sea for relief. When relief failed to come I lit a lantern, set it outside the mosquito-net close to my head, and settled back to lose myself in Borrow's "Bible in Spain." I must have read forty or fifty pages when I came to the paragraph:

> I had no sooner engaged him, than seizing the tureen of soup, which had by this time become quite cold, he placed it on top of his forefinger, or rather on the nail thereof, causing it to make various circumvolutions over his head, to my great astonishment, without spilling a drop; then springing with it to the door, he vanished, and in another moment made his appearance with the puchera, which, after a similar bound and flourish, he deposited on the table; then suffering his hands to sink before him, he put one over the other and stood at his ease with half-shut eyes, for all the world as if he had been in my service twenty years.

I laughed aloud. Little Sea grumbled in her sleep, while Desire, with wide-open, faunlike eyes, stared queerly at me. Closing my eyes I conjured up Antonio, the valet, in his bizarre guise:

> His arms were long and bony, and his whole form conveyed an idea of great activity united with no slight degree of strength; his hair was wiry, but of jetty blackness; his forehead low; his eyes small and grey, expressive of much subtlety and no less malice, strangely relieved by a strong dash of humour; the nose was handsome, but the mouth was immensely wide, and his under jaw projected considerably. A more singular physiognomy I had never seen, and I continued staring at him for some time in silence.

Suddenly I started, closed the book over my finger, and sat upright. Visions of Gipsies stealing forth on the "affairs of Egypt," of maniacs, Andalusian orange venders, and bloodthirsty robbers flashed through my mind, leaving it incapable of other thoughts. At first I knew merely that something unusual had happened: there was a new sound, like the hissing of a thousand snakes. I thought it might be the wind blowing in the fronds, but as there was still no wind, I conceived that it must be waves washing along the shore. But waves wash intermittently, while this was one long unbroken hiss. I wondered if the seas on the outer reef had increased to such an extent that they had flooded over the shallows and were even now washing across the Point. The hissing increased in volume until I imagined that a great wave must surely be rushing toward us. I sprang out of the net and ran to the door.

Complete silence; the hissing had suddenly stopped, and for a moment even the sea-birds were quiet. Then a great comber boomed along the reef, sending a seismic tremor through the islet. A frigate bird squawked, and there was a buzzing in my ears, for the mosquitoes quickly found me out.

I returned to the net and reopening "The Bible in Spain" I read on to the point where Borrow whispers the magic Gipsy words in his fractious stallion's ear:

> The Rommany Chal to his horse did cry,
> As he placed the bit in the horse's jaw;
> Kosko gry! Rommany gry!
> Muk man kistur tute knaw.

> We then rode forth from Madrid by the gate of San Vincente, directing our course to the lofty mountains which separate Old from New Castile.

Again the hiss, scarcely audible, reached my ear, coming as though from a great way off. The booming on the reef had suddenly increased to a deafening roar, but still I could hear the sibilant sound, a noise apart from the sea's roar. With increasing agitation I closed my book and shoved it under the sleeping mat. If I had had a barometer my mental state would have been explained, for the glass would have registered ominously low. Little Sea and Desire, blessed, nerveless savages, were sound asleep.

Gradually the hissing increased until I again imagined that a great wave was washing across the Point to engulf us in the lagoon. Rushing outside once more, I listened for a moment and at last understood the cause. Strangely enough, although it was dead calm where I stood, the wind was rustling overhead, carrying with it the swishing sound of the water foaming over the reef.

Then, as though it had been gathering its forces far out at sea, it struck the islet with a yell of fury, screaming through the trees, hurling fronds and nuts through the air—a force of indescribable violence, bent on destruction. Its first impact sent me staggering into the house, carried away the roof as well as the frond sides, and tore the mosquito-net from its fastenings, to whirl it, specterlike, across the lagoon.

Little Sea and Desire were safe. When I reached them they pressed their lips to my ears and shouted, simultaneously, "*Uriia!*" (Hurricane!) They were not in the least frightened; on the contrary, they seemed to be enjoying it.

I was thinking of the flying nuts and fronds and listening to the intermittent crashes as coconut-trees were snapped off and hurled to the ground. I remembered that a termite-eaten one was growing directly to windward, and no sooner had the thought come than, as though to warrant my fear, with a report like the firing of a dozen rifles the top of the tree was snapped off and hurled over our heads into the lagoon beyond.

My nerves were now keyed to a point beyond fear; nevertheless, I realized the perilousness of our situation. Matauea Point was not more than five feet above sea-level and the highest point on Ko Islet did not exceed fifteen feet. What should we do when the seas started breaking over the land itself?

We huddled together in the middle of the house, or rather in the framework of the house, with the sleeping mat to our backs. Rain came in torrents, soaking us with the first downpour. With chattering teeth I thought how nicely a pint of brandy would go down. Little Sea and Desire dozed in my arms, apparently quite comfortable.

By four in the morning the gale was at its height, blowing with such violence that we could no longer sit with our backs to it but must lie flat on the ground. Nuts, fronds, and trees had ceased falling, for most of them had long since been blown into the lagoon, and the weaker trees had gone down in the first gust. No gale can break down or uproot a sound, mature coconut-palm—it will bend its sixty-foot bole to the ground without breaking; but one log which rolled toward us with great velocity reminded me that the danger was not past. We could not see it, but we heard the crash it made when it struck a coconut stump to windward.

My mind wandered back to the story I had been reading in Borrow's "Bible in Spain." I found myself muttering over and over: "The Rommany Chal to his horse did cry," and I saw Antonio standing before me with the soup-tureen balanced on his finger-nail. He seemed to be smiling and winking at me in an incomprehensible manner. Then, yelling, he did a wild dance, tossing the tureen under his leg so that it made a turn over his head, and on the downward course he caught it in his teeth, grinning fiercely. Then, taking it on the palm of his hand he dashed it with all his strength against the stem of a coconut-palm. It bounded back without a drop lost, whereupon he caught it on the bridge of his nose and balanced it there.

Little Sea was shaking my shoulder and screaming into my ear. I was roused from my wide-awake nightmare and at length grasped the meaning of her words:

"The seas are coming! The seas are coming, Ropati!"

Dawn was breaking, a leaden, joyless dawn. I could dimly see the outlines of ragged palms with most of their fronds carried away, while the few remaining ones lay out horizontal and stiff in the mighty gale.

Then I heard a deafening roar as though the islet were being wrenched loose from its foundations and whirled to oblivion in one annihilating avalanche of

water. The next instant what remained of the house was flooded two feet deep in a foaming torrent that rushed pell-mell across the Point.

"The canoe! The canoe!" cried practical Little Sea.

Knowing that the mast stays were in the canoe, I ran out and in a moment had moored it to a coconut-palm. It was no sooner done than a second wave foamed over the Point, three feet deep. I jumped into a tree and watched the Pacific Ocean washing beneath me. Little Sea and Desire were clinging to another tree near-by.

I had not noticed in the excitement that the wind had abated and was even then diminishing by perceptible degrees. Within the next five minutes it was dead calm again. It is at such times that the seas rise, for during the height of the gale they are flattened by the wind.

The next wave took the skeleton of the little house, flooding the Point a good six feet deep. Fortunately, instead of uprooting the trees we were roosting in, it banked about two feet of sand over the whole length of the Point. But waves are fickle things, and as the next one might sweep away all the sand that had been brought in, and a good deal more besides, we took advantage of the lull between the third and fourth waves to run inland to higher ground.

It was an eerie experience watching those great seas piling over the islet, carrying débris, birds, fish, and gigantic masses of coral which had been wrenched from the reef. The two girls took advantage of every lull to jump down and gather their dresses full of the fattest fish; but I remained where I was, not wishing to put to the test of a quick scramble up the straight stem of a coconut-palm.

By midday the seas had given up their attempt to wash Danger Island into the marine ooze, leaving a tattered and torn Ko Islet strewn with dead fish, mangled trees, coral boulders, and drowned sea-birds. Then the three of us made our way slowly back to Matauea Point. I was conscious of something solid in my pocket. Pulling it out, I found that it was my copy of "The Bible in Spain." I distinctly remembered putting it under the sleeping mat, and how it managed to get into my pocket is a mystery to me to this day.

XIII

Big Stomach

"Toku matua e,
Ti yoa m'i taku yami."
Ye wakalongo tona matua,
Koa mate i te ama na Tauperoa;
Ya rere na runga
Ka Watu-manava-nui.

"Oh, Mother, come,
Bring me my yami."
The mother could not hear;
She was dead under Tauperoa's outrigger;
She had gone to the heavens
To fly with Big Stomach.

—*From* "Waiva na Watu-manava-nui" (*the chant of Big Stomach*).

Big Stomach

WILLIAM and I turned down the outer beach of Ko. The hurricane was four days past and we saw its ravages everywhere; in one place it had taken away a part of the islet and in another had filled in a bay of several acres extent. The few remaining coconut fronds hung ragged and broken against the stems of the palms; other trees were as leafless as a winter elm.

The temporary village had not been entirely wrecked, for it was on high ground in the lee of the island. Although most of the roofs were blown off, little of the copra which the Windward Islanders had been making suffered more than a good soaking. As for the main islet of Puka-Puka, the hurricane barely grazed it, doing no harm whatsoever. Even on Ko we had felt no more than the hurricane's edge, but that was quite sufficient to satisfy my curiosity with respect to tropical storms.

Tramping along a wide beach of white coral sand

cast up by the recent seas, we came to a halt near the spot where Little Sea, Desire, and I had had our picnic. From the top of the bank to a distance of a hundred yards inland was bleached gray coral, for this was the highest point on Ko and the seas had not covered it with new gravel. Seaward, the bank broke down at a steep angle to the shallows.

People seldom visit this part of the islet unless on such an errand as William's and mine: to fish for the giant milk mullet that cross the reef at high tide to bask in the shallows. In a pool three or four feet deep and some ten yards from the shore we could see a dozen of the sleek silvery creatures, each of them weighing from twenty to thirty pounds. They wallowed lazily, nibbling bits of sea grass, their dorsal fins sometimes cutting the water, sharklike. At other times they would swim close to the surface with their mouths out of water, drinking in the air. Again they would lie on the pure white sand basking like flounders.

We baited our hooks with a sea grass that grows in the lagoon, coiled the lines in our hands, and approaching the edge of the shallows threw in a quantity of chum and let our hooks sink temptingly close to the fish. Then we climbed to the top of the bank, paying out our lines, and sat down at a point where we could see the baits in limpid water.

Two immense slabs of coral were resting there, one standing upright like a gravestone, the other lying flat and fitted against the bottom of the upright one. They made a perfect seat, but when I suggested sitting there, William refused with vigorous profanity.

"What? Hell and Devil! Me sit in chair of Big Stomach? (Watu-manava-nui.) Never! Puncture me! And what's more, young man, I advise you not to sit there. He's one damn dangerous seat!"

Nevertheless, I occupied the seat, or part of it, for the great stone chair was large enough to have held four ordinary men. Each slab must have weighed at least five hundred pounds.

I turned to William, who was staring moodily at the big mullet. "This fellow Big Stomach," I suggested cautiously; "he must have been a giant to have carried these slabs here."

William snorted.

"You are one big fool, savee?" he said. "Big Stomach carried them both in one hand! You never hear about him? Devil take you! What they teach you in the white man's school?"

He adjusted his hat brim to shade his eyes, scratched his hoary bullet head, and then, after a little urging, told me the following story:

Big Stomach was the hero of Yayake, an island many days to the westward. He was born with the wings of a bird, and had eight stomachs, each of them larger than the stomach of any other superman of Yayake.

Big Stomach led his warriors in twenty double canoes to the eastward. By flying among the clouds and conversing with the winds he discovered the trackless way to Puka-Puka.

He landed on Ko Islet and there wrested the land from the Puka-Pukans, taking their wives and daughters for his warriors; and he took their sleeping mats, canoes, implements, and houses. Only two warriors withstood them: they were Tauperoa and Tokaipore, who held Matauea Point.

Big Stomach

Big Stomach made a truce with Tauperoa and Tókaipore, and for a time they all lived in peace, but hate was still in their stomachs.

The Yayake men thrived on Ko Islet. The people of the other two islets were jealous of them, but they dared not attack them. They were jealous because the Yayake men were birds of passage (*Manu wiri*), with none of the blood of Puka-Pukans in their veins, and because the foreigners had taken all the most beautiful women and held the largest of the islets. But most of all, they were jealous because these strangers feasted daily on great turtle, albacore, and sail-fish, the sweetest of all sea foods.

It was Big Stomach who fished for the Yayake men.

He placed two coral slabs on the outer beach, on the high land of Teaumaroa. There he made the seat of Big Stomach from which he could watch over the sea. There daily he gazed beyond the reef, watching for turtle and albacore.

When the great turtle came up to breathe or the sea-birds circled over the schools of albacore, Big Stomach left his coral-slab seat and flew over the sea. Soaring among the screaming birds, he watched the fish beneath him. Like a gannet he dove, and rose, dripping, carrying many albacore. He caught turtles by their tails and brought them home to his warriors.

One day he brought in three turtles and divided them among his people. But through the greed of one of his warriors an old woman, Kuma, received no share.

Kuma put on her oldest garment and bound her head with weeds; she smeared charcoal over her body, and swore all manner of vengeance against Big Stomach and his warriors. Being the daughter of kings, she could cause terror in the village.

At night she made a basket of palm fronds and waded into the lagoon. With her head hidden in the basket she swam for Matauea Point. Warriors looking over the water saw only a discarded frond basket moved by the wind toward Matauea.

Kuma went to Tauperoa and Tokaipore, the supermen of Matauea. She told them of the insult and demanded that they kill the people of Big Stomach. They promised revenge, for they hated the birdmen from Yayake.

Said Tauperoa: "But what shall we do with Kuma, for now she too is of the people of Yayake?"

Tokaipore, the bloodthirsty one, replied, laughing: "We shall kill her first, for all the Yayake must be exterminated."

Kuma fell on the ground, wailing, but the warriors' hearts were of coral. They wrenched the outrigger from their war canoe, laid it across the neck of Kuma, and, standing on either end, choked her to death.

Cried Tokaipore: "Thus shall we kill the Yayake; they are fat from much feasting, and their strength has been sapped by the women of Puka-Puka. Thus shall we strangle the foreigners!"

When the bright star Dove-of-the-morning laid its silver path to Matauea, the supermen crept softly through the groves, followed by a hundred great warriors. They crept to the village of Big Stomach, carrying the outrigger of puka-wood. At the first house in the village they pinned down the necks of the warriors, sending them back to Yayake; and thus also they strangled the women and children.

Tokaipore laughed as he watched them struggling beneath the outrigger.

A baby cried: "Oh, mother! Come, bring me my yami." The mother could not hear; she was dead under Tauperoa's outrigger. She had gone to the heavens to fly with Big Stomach.

Ten men only escaped from the village. They ran to the seat of Big Stomach and told him of the death of his people. Big Stomach gazed to westward where lay the land of his fathers. He knew that he should soon return to Yayake.

The fire clouds brightened the sea, and soon Ra the sun-god would arise. Big Stomach knew that he was doomed, for he had died that night in a dream. He rose and flew to Puka-Puka Islet, leaving the ten warriors to die to the last man.

The warriors of Puka-Puka Islet saw him soaring overhead. Hundreds of spears were thrown at him and one lodged in his ankle. Blood poured from Big Stomach's wound, and at last he fell dead in the Leeward passage.

The warriors carried his body ashore and split it open from end to end. They found that he had eight stomachs, proving that he was the greatest of men.

Big Stomach the generous! Big Stomach the birdlike! His soul has returned to Yayake. His body lies buried in the sand of Puka-Puka. Vamose! Go-ta-hell back to Yayake!

William turned his eyes toward me with a quizzical expression as though to make sure that I was not laughing at him. Then, with a yell, he grabbed the line he had wound around his toe so as to facilitate the comprehensive gestures indispensable when relating a Puka-Puka story. A thirty-pound mullet was tugging at the other end of the line. He brought the fish flopping up the embankment and sank his fanglike teeth into its head. Then the old heathen limped to Big Stomach's seat and threw the mullet in the shade of the upright slab. While rebaiting his hook he again regarded me keenly.

"Well, what do you think?" he said.

"It's a fine fish," I replied.

"Dash me! No! The story I mean."

"Oh, that's fine too."

"But it's all a lie," the old man explained, weakly.

"I believe it's true," I replied.

His eyes brightened. He scratched a hairy mole on the end of his nose before commenting in a dubious tone: "Who knows? Maybe it's got some truth in it."

"Of course it has! I think it's all true."

"I think so too!" the old man cried. "But the damn

fool missionaries say all our Puka-Puka stories are lies. But do you think it's true about Big Stomach flying?"

"Suppose he didn't fly," I said; "that doesn't mean that all the rest of the story is a lie. Perhaps at one time there was a great fisherman called Big Stomach who used to sit on this coral slab watching for turtles. And maybe, one day, he saw some large ones out at sea and became so excited that he ran bounding over the reef. Well, some children saw him and they ran to tell the others that Big Stomach jumped from the shore to the reef without touching his feet more than a dozen times. When the story was repeated, many people said, more than likely, that Big Stomach jumped from the shore to the reef without touching his feet more than once, and finally, that he had jumped from his seat into the sea at one great leap. Maybe that is how the story started, and after Big Stomach's death it grew and grew until people believed that he really flew and was so strong that he carried these coral slabs here in one hand."

Old William glanced keenly at me.

"Hmm!" he grunted, and that was his only comment.

Some weeks later while we were walking on the main islet, William showed me the grave of Big Stomach. It was sixteen feet long by five wide. The headstone was chiseled to represent a bird, and on either side of the grave were four large slabs of coral to represent his eight fabulous stomachs.

XIV

Wail-of-Woe's Marriage

Teiake te pirip'u o te ropa,
Ya kanapanapa pe te io o te turama,
Na makeke pe te kiri o te mango,
Na mumura pe te reva o Viggo
Ya wakatere ki te ekeonga a Yato.

Here are the trousers for the bridegroom,
Bright like a lamp chimney,
Strong like a shark's skin,
Red like Viggo's flag
When he rounds the Leeward Point.

—*From* "Mako no te Akamaata" (*chant to the bridegroom*).

Wail-of-Woe's Marriage

WHEN I first came to Puka-Puka the house on the west side of the trading-station was occupied by old man Breadfruit (Kuru), his wife and family. One of his children was a tall thin lad named Wail-of-Woe (Tangi). He was given this name because at the time of his birth neighbors were wailing over the body of a dead baby. Thus most native names are acquired. A man may be called Sickness (Maki)—a common name—because of some illness in the family at the time of his birth. Likewise he may be called Blind Eyes (Mata-Po) in memory of a blind relative; Many Fish (Eikarai) in honor of a father or an uncle who had lately brought in a record catch of albacore. Little Sea got her name from her mother, who, being born aboard a schooner, was called Great Sea (Moana-rai). When they named Desire there must have been a presentiment as to the bewitching little creature she was to become.

As I have said, Wail-of-Woe was thin. He coughed

frequently, and I soon realized that he was consumptive—in other words, doomed, for I have never known a Puka-Pukan to survive tuberculosis. Two thirds of the deaths on the islands are caused by this terrible disease.

Nevertheless, Wail-of-Woe attended the love fests and soon found the girl of his heart, one Sun-Eater (Kaira), the unwieldy daughter of a Gilbert Islander, Rock Grouper (Tarau) by name.

My first intimation of the match was when Rock Grouper came into the store to spend a carefully hoarded bag of money on trousers, shirt, arm-bands, red necktie, green hat-ribbon, a bottle of scent, and Boston garters for his intended son-in-law. It is the island custom for the bride's relatives to clothe the groom, while the latter's relatives dress the bride.

Later in the day Breadfruit came into the store with some of his kin and purchased a great quantity of finery for Sun-Eater: ribbons, calico, Jap lace, Swiss embroidery, and yards and yards of white muslin.

On the day of the wedding Little Sea came to me in a great flurry of excitement. Wail-of-Woe and Sun-Eater were going to the church and she wanted me to see them pass. Wail-of-Woe walked ahead, very stiff and self-conscious in all his new clothes and some borrowed ones as well. His red necktie and the green ribbon wound many times around George's bowler hat were very conspicuous—almost as much so as his Boston garters, which had been attached outside the legs of his trousers, and as there were no socks to support, the ends flapped rhythmically against his bony legs. He had also borrowed Abel's squeaking shoes for the occasion.

Sun-Eater walked demurely a modest distance behind, her comfortable girth increased by twenty yards of muslin and a dozen chemises borrowed from her relatives. Her dress reached to the ground and lay in folds and ruffles about her person so that only her chubby face and the tips of her fingers were visible. It was a dress to gladden the hearts of the missionaries. Perched on top of her head was a pandanus-leaf hat decorated with polychromatic ribbons and streamers, including two red-and-black typewriter ribbons that I had contributed.

Little Sea and I followed the crowd to the church, and after Sea Foam had duly spliced the couple in the presence of the assembled community including scores of naked urchins who filled all the church windows, laughing and cracking more or less obscene jokes, Wail-of-Woe and his wife repaired to Breadfruit's house, where they sat stiffly on a mat placed before the door.

Then the fun began. With the whoop of a Filipino gone amuck, Rock Grouper, the bride's father, rushed from his house across the street with an old singlet in one hand and two yards of dungaree in the other.

Stopping before the married couple, he did an extemporaneous dance to the accompaniment of a weird Gilbert Island song. Then, holding the singlet and dungaree aloft, he yelled: "This is a day of great sadness! Gaze at these, O people of Puka-Puka! A new singlet which cost me twelve shillings" (I had sold it to him six months before for three), "and all thrown away on this worthless, good-for-nothing, ugly imbecile Wail-of-Woe!"

Here, to my astonishment, Wail-of-Woe nodded his head sympathetically, apparently in full accord with his father-in-law's aspersions.

With another whoop Rock Grouper continued: "This marriage is none of my doing! I have been against it from the first! Yes, people of Puka-Puka, for years I absolutely refused to let my fine fat daughter marry this ne'er-do-well. Look at her, people of Puka-Puka! She has the royal blood of Peru Island in her stomach; a finer, fatter woman is not to be found—and all, all thrown away on the worthless idiot, Wail-of-Woe! Curse him, the bag of bones! Not only does he steal my beautiful daughter, but likewise he bleeds me of my substance! See! The very clothes on his back—it was I who bought them, for I was ashamed, knowing that otherwise he would come naked to the wedding! And now he greedily takes my beautiful singlet too! *Aué!* My beautiful twelve-shilling singlet!"

With that he furiously threw the ragged singlet at Wail-of-Woe, crying, "Gone are my beautiful twelve-shilling singlet and my fine fat daughter! *Aué!* I am now a pauper!"

Again Wail-of-Woe nodded sympathetically. Rock Grouper was working himself into a frenzied state. Tears were actually flowing down his cheeks. Hundreds of people had gathered about, and all nodded sympathetically.

I felt sorry for Wail-of-Woe, but, as I soon learned, my sympathy was wasted.

After another harangue further disparaging Wail-of-Woe and extolling his daughter to the skies, Rock Grouper flung the two yards of dungaree at the bridegroom and retired.

Then came Breadfruit, as speedily as his elephantiasis legs would permit. Six yards of cheap print cloth streamed from one hand, and in the other was a rat-gnawed pair of women's stockings.

"This is a day of great sorrow!" he yelled. "Weep with me, people of Puka-Puka, for to-day a penniless woman, old enough to be his mother, has stolen, no less than stolen, my son! I absolutely forbade the match, for years I forbade it, but at last the tears of Sun-Eater's family softened my heart, and I reluctantly consented to this unnatural marriage. Look at her! A mere Gilbert Island savage! It was I, Breadfruit, who bought every yard of cloth on her back; without me she would have come naked to the marriage! I was ashamed, so I threw away the savings of years to clothe the hussy! Look at her great mouth that would frighten a shark! Her hair is falling out with old age, and she hasn't a tooth in her head! And gaze upon my noble son, the flower of the young men of Puka-Puka, thrown away upon this hideous Gilbert Island cannibal!"

At this Sun-Eater nodded sympathetically, as did the rest of the inhabitants.

With many a despairing grunt, Breadfruit moved feebly through the steps of a dance, and then, flinging the stockings at the bride, he screamed: "Now I am a pauper! Everything is taken, these beautiful stockings, my son—all, all is thrown away on this loose woman!" With that he sank to the ground, weeping, at the same time throwing the print cloth at Sun-Eater, claiming that it cost four shillings a yard (only a few hours before I had sold it to him at ninepence).

Thus went the ceremony of "Making Big" (*Akamaata*). Bosun-Woman, of whom I shall have more to say, came next. She was past her day and ugly, but she held the audience in suspense for ten minutes with an indelicate song and dance. Then she gave the bridegroom a box of matches and danced off into the crowd.

With a whoop and a wild waving of his arms, George, the dandy, sprang before the couple flourishing a bottle of hair-oil and yelling that it had cost him eighteen shillings (every one knew that one and sixpence was the price, but that mattered nothing). However, he, George, son of the exceptional man whose name was Abraham, and of the woman from Windward Village known to be one of the daughters of the redoubtable Ura, chief of police and deacon of the church—he, the generous George, cared nothing for expense; he was more than willing to buy costly gifts for Sun-Eater, for, he admitted, he knew her rather intimately, having won her maiden love years ago. He added that he had generously given her her freedom when he found that poor old Wail-of-Woe wanted to marry her.

Then he buttoned his overcoat closely about him—he was never without it at public functions—took from Wail-of-Woe's head the bowler hat he had loaned him, put it on his own head, threw the bottle of hair-oil into Sun-Eater's lap, and strode off at a manly gait.

Old Mama came next. She was waving a handkerchief over her head. (I had sold it to her that morning for ninepence; the real price was a shilling, but it was somewhat shopworn.) Mama screamed that it was no ordinary handkerchief, but a particularly fine one that her friend the trader had brought from Cowboyland, and that the trader had reluctantly parted with it for nine shillings; all of which, she added, was quite thrown away on Wail-of-Woe. Nevertheless, as a matter of family pride, she felt it her duty to give it to him. She then put her withered limbs through a hula-hula and departed.

So the ceremony proceeded. Little Sea and Desire offered their presents, lying as outrageously as the rest, and I presented a bag of flour. When I turned away without "Making Big," Benny jumped up and spoke in my stead, bouncing the price of the flour to as many pounds as it was shillings. Then old William joined him, and together they disparaged the bride and groom with equal venom, at the same time exalting me to the sky. They closed with the inevitable song and dance.

"There!" said Benny, coming to me; "if I hadn't spoken they would have thought that was only an ordinary fifteen-shilling bag of flour."

"So it was," I replied. Benny gave me an astonished glance.

"But it isn't now!" he said, and I think he believed it.

Many brought presents of roast chickens and pigs, swinging the fowls by the legs as they extolled their succulence. Others brought drinking nuts, fish and taro cooked into puddings (*oro-vai-kai*).

When evening had set in, the food was divided so that every one who had taken part in the ceremony should receive a share. But the other presents were kept by the newly-weds, although, at some marriages, even these are divided. Thus, if a man attends a marriage and gives the bridegroom a pair of trousers, he may very well take them home with him again, or perhaps a pair of women's stockings in place of them. At this type of "Making Big," George invariably gives his army overcoat with the understanding that, when the division comes, it will be returned to him. This presentation of Puka-Puka's most sumptuous piece of apparel is a long, noisy, and tearful ceremony, always attended by great excitement.

II

That night Little Sea was thoughtful. All at once she jumped up and cried: "Ropati! Let's you and I get married!"

Desire was lounging on a mat at one side. She clapped her hands in hearty agreement with this proposal.

"All right, I'm willing," I said. "But why do you want to get married? We are happy enough as it is."

"Te apinga! Te apinga!" squealed Desire.

"Oh, so that's it! You want a grand 'Making Big,' so that you will get all sorts of things, like Sun-Eater. But she got nothing but a lot of old stockings and worthless dresses."

"Yes," said Little Sea; "but she had a fine time getting them."

"Is that your only reason for wanting to get married?"

"Yes."

"Very well, then, we'll be married to-morrow."

And so we were. Sea Foam tied the knot; then came the great gift-giving ceremony. It was much the same as Wail-of-Woe's, so I will not describe it except to say that among other presents I received George's army overcoat, King-of-the-Sky's vivid green, brass-buttoned coat, and old William's hat brim. During the presentation of these articles the groves reverberated with yells and groans, and I was afterward told that it was the greatest spectacle seen, or heard, on Puka-Puka within the memory of the oldest inhabitant.

III

This is, perhaps, as good a place as another in which to speak of Puka-Puka house-building, for it is shortly after his marriage that a man prepares to build for his family a permanent coral-lime house.

This is quite an undertaking, requiring far-sighted

plans that strain the profound Puka-Puka mind to the utmost. First of all, one must obtain a pig and fatten him for two or more years, and must so arrange matters that when the pig is full grown the wife will have plenty of taro ready to be eaten. If there is no taro when the pig is ready, he is then killed and a young pig is procured. Arrangements must then be made to insure a supply of taro by the time the second pig is grown.

This food is for those who help the house-builder, for usually the whole village takes an active part, most of them sitting in the shade, generously giving the builder advice, while a few of the more foolish ones assist with the mere manual part of the labor.

The initial work is to dig a pit eight feet by eight and six deep. This is filled with dry wood, coconut logs, etc., and on top are piled a hundred or more great slabs of coral. When this work is finished the wood is lighted, the pig is killed, the taro made into pudding, and every one has a grand feast while the coral is being burnt into lime.

The husband then deserves, and takes, a long rest: a year or more is needed for recuperation and for talking over plans for the house. It may very well be that the married couple have no need for a house, for their father's house is large enough for all. But the children—yes, they must leave a suitable dwelling for their children. All natives feel a strong sense of obligation toward their children and this is fully met by building for their future occupancy a coral-lime house. I often hear them speaking of their children, whether or no they have any; for, if they have none, they adopt some from a more fortunate neighbor. On Puka-Puka such adopted children are regarded exactly as though they were the flesh and blood of their foster-parents.

After his period of rest, the house-builder sets to work gathering more coral blocks. This requires a year or more, and when enough have been assembled another pig is killed and more taro cooked for the helpers.

Then comes a period that may cover any number of years during which the builder chips his blocks into squares suitable for building the walls of his house. On some nights he may chip as much as a whole block; on rare occasions as many as two. Usually he chips no more than the side of one, and often many nights pass in succession when no work at all is done.

By the time the blocks are all ready the husband will have been married a number of years and has become the father of an increasing family, either adopted children or his own. He now rests for a year or two, deciding that on a certain New Year's Day he will start erecting the sides of his house. Meanwhile, when the time approaches, he discovers that the thatch-roof of his so-called temporary abode is leaking and that he must have a new one. So he delays work on the new house until he can re-roof the old one—that is, his father's house, where he is sojourning for the time being.

It is quite possible that by this time ten years have elapsed. Several of his children are going to school;

like most of his neighbors he has become a deacon of the church; he is in rotund, contented middle life; it would be foolish to spoil the serenity of his life with too much work.

Nevertheless, he at length goes to work with a will, for he has children who must not be left homeless. He fattens two more pigs. When, in the twelfth year, they are ready, the villagers gather again with advice while he cuts down trees from which to make rafters, doors, and window-frames. When these have been made the pigs are killed and all join in another feast.

No further work can be done, of course, until more pigs have been fattened, and somewhere about the fourteenth year this deficiency is supplied. Thereupon the villagers gather as before, and one side of the house is erected.

"Ah!" sighs the father, virtuously, "there shall be a house for my children when I am gone!" and with this he ceases to worry and rests for another year.

Fifteen years have now slipped by and his oldest daughter is attending the love fests. She will marry soon. The father realizes that haste is necessary, so he starts feeding another pig. But at the end of seventeen years the eldest daughter decides to get married, so this pig is sacrificed for the wedding feast and the house-building still further delayed.

Then another new roof is needed for his temporary house—his own now, for his father has died. Then his eldest son decides to marry, so again the pigs are sacrificed, and the house waits for its second wall until the twenty-first year.

The father now observes that he is getting on in years; but never say die! If he lives to a ripe old age he may yet finish all four walls of his house; and it is now his married son's duty to re-roof the old house, and only a few of the children are left to be married.

When at last the house is finished it will be of no use to his children (except, of course, as a temporary abode), for they are now all married and have long since started building coral-lime houses of their own. They too are now saying that it is a man's duty to prepare a house for his children.

Thus the inhabitants of Puka-Puka live always in temporary houses, merely stopping there for the brief period of their lives until their own houses are ready.

XV

Jeffrey and Bosun, Ltd.

Koa roa to mateinga,
Yeke koe ko na vaka Atua,
Raua koe e Iitu
Ma te paparangi
Te ruru tane Maroroyi.

You have now been long dead,
You have gone away in the canoe of the god,
You and the night-god Iitu,
To the farthermost land of the earth,
To Maroroyi, land of the strong men.

—*From* "Mako no te Mateinga" (*a Puka-Pukan death chant*).

Jeffrey and Bosun, Ltd.

THEY are great friends, Wail-of-Woe and Bosun-Woman (Posini-Wawine). Wail-of-Woe has now been married a year and is in the last stages of consumption. Bosun-Woman visits him daily, as does her husband, Jeffrey (Tiavare), for the woman is the village undertaker, while her husband is the doctor.

Loud-mouthed Bosun-Woman! None of Walter Scott's old women who hobble to wakes could surpass her in ghoulishness. She takes a morbid pleasure in the visits of the grim reaper, goes into ecstasies over a nicely laid-out corpse, screeching out her own praises when she manages a death in perfect island fashion. She is not far past forty but appears much older, except for her hair, which is still black. It lies loosely down her back in tangled hanks, damp with fish-oil—cold clammy locks like those of a long-buried corpse. Her cheeks are flabby, her eyes bloodshot, and her mouth large, white, and bloodless. She is always smiling, a horrible smile, as though she were thinking of the next corpse she would lay out and of the revel she would have, wailing over the departed. Often when I have been under the weather she has smiled thus at me, as though to cheer me with the thought that it would be no less than a pleasure for her to prepare the body of a white man for burial.

Her husband, Jeffrey, is much older than herself. He is tall, bony, and walks with a wriggling motion as though his hips were out of joint. He shaves every Christmas with the Central Village razor. At other times his hirsute jowls bristle with a pepper-and-salt beard, each hair as thick as baling-wire. His is the most self-esteeming leer I have ever seen. He wears a grass skirt, nothing else. Ah, yes, and he is building a coral-lime house for the children of childless Bosun-Woman.

Jeffrey, as I have said, is the village doctor. He mixes noxious things like fish intestines, chicken droppings, coconut bark, sea urchins, and other rubbish, for all known diseases of man or beast, external or internal. These he administers in large doses, and if the patient is not immediately cured by the power of suggestion, he dies from the effect of the medicine.

Jeffrey has three other methods of treatment. One is massage (*tarome*), which is often helpful. The second is by invocations to the spirits of the dead, who, he claims, cause the patient's illness by possessing his body. Thus a deceased blind grandfather will cause sore eyes in his granddaughter as a kind of revenge or compensation for his own trouble on earth. Also, Jeffrey declares, a dead father who had been afflicted with yaws will possess his son's body, causing the disease in a new generation. The father wishes his son to know what he suffered in life so that the son may sympathize. But in many cases Jeffrey's invocations cure, for they create a hopeful state of mind in the sick person, who believes that the malignant spirit is being driven out.

The third method of cure is disastrous in most cases, particularly tuberculosis, for it consists in putting the patient on a strict diet of a very coarse species of taro (*puraka*), land crabs, and coconut crabs. Jeffrey claims that by eating fish, birds, good taro, coconuts, eggs, fowls, and the like, the effect of his medicine is neutralized. This taboo comes doubtless from ancient times, when the witch doctors shrewdly killed off the weaklings in an effort to combat overpopulation. The taboo also saved the fish and taro for the strong warriors and the witch doctors themselves. How such a taboo came into effect can easily be imagined. In a communistic form of government, when the fishing was poor or the taro crop scant, it was undoubtedly a temptation to omit the shares of the unfit who were unable to produce any food. Compassion for invalids and old people exists only among civilized people, and even there it is seldom more than a reflex of self-compassion.

Wail-of-Woe sank fast on his diet of *puraka* and crabs, as well as from his daily doses of nauseous medicine. I did not interfere, for there was not the slightest hope of saving him, and it seemed more humane to let him slip quickly from his misery.

On visiting Wail-of-Woe, Bosun-Woman would amuse herself by composing the death chant she intended to wail over him. In addition to this there would also be all the ancient chants. Sometimes Wail-of-Woe would make suggestions or improvements in a verse or two; and often he would discuss with her the arrangements for the burial—how many yards of calico would suffice for a respectable winding-sheet, etc. To me all this was morbid in the extreme, but Wail-of-Woe seemed to have no fear of the approaching end.

One evening Little Sea came to tell me that Wail-of-Woe would die that night. She said Jeffrey had said so and that all the relatives had arrived to wait for his last breath, so that they might start the death wail. She was right: he would die, for no native can live after such a suggestion from the witch doctor.

With an unpleasant sensation creeping up and down my spine I went to Wail-of-Woe's house and looked in. He was sitting in Sea Foam's steamer chair, while close by sat a dozen people staring silently at him. His eyes were round and hollow, and his body frightfully emaciated.

"I'm going to die to-night, Ropati," he muttered hoarsely, and then broke down with a racking fit of coughing.

Bosun-Woman was not there; it was not proper for her to appear until after the first death wail—but she was wide awake at home, waiting.

The sick man's mother sobbed, Sun-Eater chanted part of a death song, and then all was silent except for Breadfruit, who puffed asthmatically on a pandanus-leaf cigarette.

I returned to the trading-station in an agitated frame of mind. I put an airy record on my phonograph and then quickly stopped the thing, for it occurred to me that Wail-of-Woe would certainly hear it and contrast the joys of living with the cold unconsciousness of death; but no doubt I gave him credit for more imagination than he possessed.

About two in the morning I woke with a start. A piercing screech rent the air, sending a shiver along my nerves.

"Wail-of-Woe is dead," Little Sea muttered, sitting upright. I grasped and held her tightly while screech after screech cut through the still night air.

Hurrying footsteps sounded on the road below. I moved to the window and looked out. Bosun-Woman was going to the wake; the moon shone full on her flabby face; her ghastly smile was broader than ever and her lips moved as she refreshed her memory by repeating lines of the new death chant. She walked with a light mincing step and her hair slapped back and forth across her back like a wet rag.

Others followed: children, old men, old women, all on their way to hear the new dirge which Bosun-Woman would wail over the body of her dead friend.

Soon the screeching subsided and the death chant burst forth like a banshee's wail of grief. But how is one to describe the death chant of the Puka-Pukans, with nothing of the sort from civilized lands to be used as a comparison? It is peculiar to the island, and nowadays such chants have been largely forgotten elsewhere in the Pacific. It is moaned in a guttural tone and broken by sporadic wails and eerie arpeggios when least expected. It rises slowly into ear-splitting crescendos when the wife throws herself across the body of her husband, tearing her hair, with outcries that chill the blood—then it sinks as slowly to a murmured, whispered requiem, when even the coconut-shell fire seems to burn more dimly and the shapes of the mourners vanish into the shadows, leaving the dead man, bound in his white winding-sheet, in vivid relief. The monotony of the meter lends a weird fascination, until one finds one's self unconsciously swaying the body in unison with Bosun-Woman, uttering meaningless syllables in her unvarying cadence.

When I first heard it a strange sensation came over me; I thought I was losing my mind, for its sobbing intonation seemed to come from another world. I dashed my hands against my head to bring myself out from under its spell.

All that night, all the next day, and all the following night Bosun-Woman led the death chant over the body of Wail-of-Woe. Thus they exhausted themselves emotionally, abandoning themselves to grief until an inevitable reaction set in; so that when Wail-of-Woe was finally buried, even Sun-Eater could meet the world with a smile. Possibly people more highly civilized mourn longer over their dead because they suppress the outward manifestation of their emotions. At Puka-Puka sorrow is exaggerated to such an extent that an early reaction is bound to come.

Over the body of Wail-of-Woe they chanted:

Te ngutu mumura e rere na,
Te arero e t'u pe te aui.
Toku mouri, toku yana tane,
I raro i te tanu ko te po et'i
Ke piri taua, pe rua wetu rangi
Ke manea taua taratara ko te rangi.

The red lips are flying about,
The tongue as fierce as the fire.
Pupils of my eyes, my gift-man,
Beneath a single gravestone
We shall lie clasped; like two stars
We shall converse in the heavens,

and so on for hundreds of verses in most of which the similes and metaphors are so obscure that only a native with a complete knowledge of Polynesian mythology and local legends could understand them. The above stanza is comparatively clear: the first two lines signify that the news of Wail-of-Woe's death is being cried through the villages. The two metaphors in the third line are common Puka-Puka idioms. "Pupils of my eyes" means the person I am always gazing at until his image has become fixed in my pupils. The second, "my gift-man," means the person I am unworthy of and could never have gained through my own efforts, but who has come to me like a gift.

Toward the end of the chant is a caustic allusion to the hypothetical woman who may have been making love to Sun-Eater's husband on the sly. Bosun-Woman led Sun-Eater in the wail:

Te ngutu o te pirara!
Kiri mata huri-huri;
Eje takere kite yua,
Te pakuongi na kalaponga!
Eje maraia pipiro!
E wuwuri kio kawalolao,
E lal 'o m'i Ayau Kava—
E! kokoti toku manako, E! E! E!

The mouth of the vixen!
Eyelids black and speckled;
She never bathes her body.
Her cheeks are caked with filth!
I hate the smelling one!
But I am strong in the taro rows,
I dig the taro of Ajau Kava—
Alas! my thoughts are broken, alas! alas! alas!

Again Bosun-Woman led the dirge in metaphors odd to Western ears (I omit the native version):

My upright tree has fallen;
It had grown straight, clean, and well rounded.
It was oily, it was glossy,
It had become a powerful hero.
A flash extinguished like the lightning.
From his black hair my desire sprung;
But now my tree has fallen;
It had grown straight, clean, and well rounded,
Far in the groves; I admired it,
For there had risen the man of Taga,
Like the fire, like the coral pass,
A flash extinguished like the lightning.

At times Sun-Eater would rise, stand with her legs astraddle her dead husband, and wail an obscene chant while her body writhed in a dance of the most salacious symbolism. But to the mourners there was nothing indecent about it; it was a demonstration of great love, for Sun-Eater was debasing herself to show that now nothing mattered, that since the death of Wail-of-Woe she was but a worm without self-respect or any desire to make herself attractive to others.

I have a collection of thousands of verses from Puka-Puka songs of the dead, and they are but a small part of all the existing songs, both ritual and legendary. They will soon be forgotten, for the natives are taught by the missionaries that there is no history worth remembering but biblical history. Although the legendary history of Puka-Puka is far more veracious than that of friends Jonah, Adam, Noah, *et al.,* and of no more concupiscent a nature than that of Lot and his daughters, Ammon, Solomon, and a host of other biblical libertines; nevertheless, the London Missionary Society regards it with the greatest abhorrence, discouraging in every conceivable manner its retention by the natives.

There is much genuine history in the chants. There are references to the Great Migration, genealogies of kings and warriors, the story of the digging of the first taro-beds, of voyages to other islands, and in one of them is the complete chronicle of the arrival of the first foreign ship. It tells how the warriors wrapped themselves in their armor of sennit and went apprehensively aboard the ship. Then it describes minutely the things they saw, with a wealth of detail wherein everything from the cook's ladle to the cat's-eye is described by a curious comparison to some article known to the Puka-Pukans. The chant ends with a decision to build a ship for a voyage to Tahiti and then to Rarotonga, where

> We shall divide a great tract of land
> And plant it with bananas—
> Full of bananas the foreign land,
> Full of plantains and taro.

But I have dwelt overlong on the foolish songs of a foolish people, and although they are semi-historical, they can have but little interest for any one except an anthropologist, a Puka-Pukan, or myself. It has been a temptation to ramble on, for this island is perhaps the last of all the Pacific galaxy to retain a few of the immemorial customs of Polynesia. Another generation and it too will fall before the inexorable invasion of the Philistines. *Sic transit gloria mundi.* They may as well exterminate the race while about it, for without their own traditions, their own centuries-old customs, what remains for a race, whether civilized or primitive, white, black, or brown?

XVI

Letter and Table-Salt

Na akaruke koe i t'u tane pe te murare?
Ki apaioio 'u ki te wui tane?
I t'ia n'i e rima ke te toe kaokao,
E rima ke te toe kaokao.

Do you throw me away like a fool?
Do I gape at men and women?
Now two wives I shall have:
One for each arm.

—*From* "Mako Akaturi" (*a Puka-Puka cuckold's lament*).

Letter and Table-Salt

LETTER and Table-Salt (Rata and Miti) are half-witted deaf-mutes, the sons of Bones, a lecherous old man who plays amorous strains on a mouth organ and is always snooping about the outer beach at night, spying on the young people at the love fests. They had a sister called Purotu (Fair Maiden), who was one of the most remarkable monstrosities I have ever laid eyes on. She was about eighteen and measured nearly as much horizontally as vertically. Her face was as flat as a map of landless seas and even more expressionless. She dressed invariably in a grass skirt, which increased her girth enormously and dragged on the ground, so that as she moved along the village street one was horribly fascinated by the sight of a half-naked body resting on a movable haycock.

Fair Maiden spent most of her time in the lagoon, for she was even more amphibious than the rest of the islanders. There, alone, she wallowed ducklike along the surface, mysteriously buoyed up until it seemed that the naked half of her was always out of water, but it was no nymphlike apparition to impassion lonely fishermen. I have known her to sleep, floating on the lagoon, and sometimes she spent the entire night paddling and drowsing in the water, more than likely ending her voyages at one of the far islets. One evening not long ago, while paddling across the lagoon, I nearly ran my canoe into her. She "sounded" like a bonito and must have remained a long time under water, for I saw no more of her.

She ate her fish raw, head, bones, scales, and all, her only other food being coconuts. She would take a coconut out into the lagoon with her, wrench some shell-fish from the coral, and dine to her heart's content, afterward taking a floating siesta. When ashore she followed her father, Bones, about like a dog, whining if she lost sight of him; but in the water she needed no guardian. A short time ago she disappeared—where, no one knows. Like the fish of the sea she died, her death unseen, and no doubt she was dined upon by the relatives of the sea creatures which she herself had eaten for so long—all of which was no more than fair.

Her brothers, Letter and Table-Salt, are as peculiar in their own way as Fair Maiden was in hers. Letter dresses in a flaming red skull-cap, a sailcloth shirt mottled with little pieces of colored cloth in diamonds, hearts, and crosses, and a pair of dungaree trousers. He has sewn innumerable pockets on his trousers, for he is much of an old maid, and in each pocket he

keeps one of his treasures. Thus he has one for his matches, one for his tobacco, and pockets respectively for his picture handkerchief, his marbles, fish-hooks, popgun, pictures torn from my discarded magazines, and one for his stemless pipe, which he sucks as though it were an egg.

Table-Salt dresses more simply in a pair of old duck trousers chopped off at the knee. He decorates himself with gardenias, wandering every afternoon along the taro-beds where the bushes grow, gathering large quantities of the flowers, which he sticks into his bushy hair until he is decked out with blossoms like a peach-tree in spring. Often he makes long wreaths to hang about his neck. Then he strolls through the villages, usually meeting Letter by the coral wall inclosing the churchyard. This is only a few yards from my trading-station, so I often witness their encounters.

The two brothers hate each other, and although they can only utter meaningless, scarcely human sounds, they hold long arguments and express themselves by pantomime. Letter is a misogynist and a sadist in intent. Table-Salt is a seducer of women, also only in intent. Neither of them has ever known a woman's love, which is doubtless why such souls as they may have have grown so strangely distorted.

When Benny and I hear them "wä-wäing" we often walk out to have a chat with them. Table-Salt will go through a pantomimic description of how he has seduced one of the village virgins, explaining with such minute gesticulatory details that even old William would blush to see them. Then Letter will exhibit his tiny muscles and explain with fire and fury how he bound some woman to a tree and flogged her till morning. The veins stand out on his forehead as he describes how he wound the imagined hair of his victim about his fingers and wrists and dragged her to the tree where he beat her until he was exhausted.

They are a sweet family, the Boneses—the salacious-minded old father and his two imbecile sons. But they have helped me to pass many a dreary evening. When I have nothing else to look forward to, I can at least promise myself a few moments' diversion by listening to the nightly altercation of Letter and Table-Salt, standing by to part the brothers when Letter brags about how he has just come from the murder of Table-Salt's favorite mistress.

XVII

Sea Foam's Treasure Larder

Kii toku wale i te Ra-Nauanga,
Te poki, te puaka, e te kai papaa.
Akaputu ya tamawine i te pa
Ya umere i te umukai waro.

My house is full on Christmas,
The poki, the pig, and the foreign food.
All the maidens gather about the door
Astonished at my great feast.

—*From* "Mako Ra-Nauanga" (*Christmas chant*).

Sea Foam's Treasure Larder

WHEN Viggo left me on Puka-Puka I gave little thought to my personal provisions. The captain urged me to supply myself generously from the schooner's stock of tinned food, but I had done so sparingly, believing that I could live almost entirely on native food. I remembered having "gone native" on Tahiti; but I had forgotten that there had always been a few pounds of sugar in the house, that every morning a Chinese baker had brought me bread, and that Tahiti is rich in foods unknown on a coral atoll.

So I started living on a semi-native diet, with the addition of sugar, coffee, bread and butter, onions, and a few other delicacies of the sort. Leeward Village agreed to supply me with native food. I paid them two pounds ten shillings a month (I still do), in return for which they brought me an abundance of fish and taro, occasionally a chicken or a bunch of bananas, and six drinking-coconuts a day. The forty men of the village took turns fishing for me. Sometimes they would bring me an albacore, some days lobsters and other shell-fish, milk mullet, or a fat sea eel. On the first Sunday in each month I would roast a young pig and on other Sundays a fowl.

Thus, with eggs, at sixpence a dozen, coffee, and bread and butter, I lived well enough for more than four months. But one morning when I sat down to my coffee I found that the sugar bag was empty. A few days later I scraped the last of the butter from my last tin. Then when bread-making day came I realized that I could not make yeast without sugar. I took the matter philosophically at first, for I wanted to prove to myself that I could live comfortably without imported foods. But it was useless. When, at length, the coffee gave out I was in a miserable state. In the morning I would fry some unleavened dough and try to convince myself that I enjoyed the rubbery stuff; at noon, after eating taro and fish to repletion, I would rise from the table unsatisfied. I felt constantly the need of sugar. One day this want became so acute that I went to the government house, where a few medicines were stored, and sucked the sugar coating from two hundred Dover powder pills. Unluckily (or luckily), they were only sugar-coated ones. I afterward obtained a sugar substitute by tapping coconut buds after the manner in which toddy is made; but this did not occur to me until just before Viggo's return.

I had been without coffee for a month, when one day I mentioned the fact to Sea Foam. The worthy

preacher scratched his head thoughtfully for some time; then he rose with a magnanimous smile and, crooking his index-finger, motioned me to follow him. He led me into a dingy room of the mission-house, opened a back door to let in the light, and started rummaging through a dozen old packing-cases.

Presently he rose from his knees, holding a rust-eaten tin in his hand. On the label, age-worn and faded, I read: "Van Camp's Pork and Beans." If the parson had produced a bowl of goldfish from his shirt-sleeve it could not have surprised me more. My mouth watered, my fingers tingled as I reached for it.

Sea Foam shook his head in a very decided way. "No," he said, "this is not coffee; this is a tin of beans. Now let me see: it must have been the white missionary, Mr. Judson, in Papua, who gave me this tin nine years ago when I was going up-river to preach to some cannibals. It makes a fine decoration for my table on Christmas when we Puka-Pukans load our tables with food and then walk through the village to see who has got the best Christmas dinner."

After another dive into the packing-case, Sea Foam brought forth a tin of American butter. It was red with rust, but I could still make out the label. After fondling the tin for a moment, Sea Foam said: "Yes, it was the Reverend Johns who gave this to my father many years ago during his first visit to the island. I remember that he brought two tins ashore. He ate one and left the other for my father."

One by one Sea Foam produced relics from the white man's civilization as though he were unearthing antiques of a vanished race—archaic bronzes or amphoræ. There were tins of soup, milk, succotash, a package of tea covered with the mold of years, a tin of stewed prunes, some cape oysters, a bag containing what had once been oatmeal—bottles and cartons from which the labels had long since disappeared.

I stared in astonishment at these decayed provisions. "Why haven't you eaten these things, Sea Foam," I said, "instead of letting them spoil?"

"Eat them!" the parson cried. "And what earthly good would they be to me if I ate them? No! Never would I eat them! No house in Puka-Puka can show such wealth as mine, and on Christmas day every one envies me when they see all these fine foods spread on my table."

"And it's not safe," he went on, "to eat these foreign foods. Once, I remember, a doctor who came with Captain McCullough in the *Sea Maiden*, gave me a box of some kind of candy. They were little things about half as big as a marble, and were coated with chocolate, but inside they were very bitter. The doctor said they were to be eaten when one had pains in the stomach. Well, I ate them all one afternoon and they nearly killed me. I was so sick that I couldn't preach my sermon the next day. No, Ropati-Cowboy, these things are all very well to put on my table at Christmas time, but I shall never again eat any of the white man's food."

He pulled a dusty gunny-sack from one of the packing-cases. "Ah, this is the coffee," he said.

I seized the bag eagerly, broke the twine, and looked

in. It was half-full of hoary berries that must have lain in the mission-house for at least a decade. Nevertheless, I took a cupful home, roasted it, ground it, and made a potful of coffee as black as sin and as strong as old man Jackson's mule.

I drank cup after cup and then sank back with the sensation of having eaten my first square meal in months. It was a delicious beverage, by far the finest coffee that I have ever tasted. My long period of abstinence may have had something to do with my relish for it, but my conclusion was that coffee, like brandy, improves with age. The new supply I received on Viggo's return seemed tasteless stuff in comparison with Sea Foam's archaic brand.

That night Little Sea wondered why I wouldn't let her sleep. I sat up in the mosquito-net, telling her stories of Cowboyland, of Buffalo Bill (who had metamorphosed into myself), and other absurd tales of hair-raising adventure. I discovered on this occasion that a "coffee jag" is something more than a myth.

XVIII

Mr. Withers—Resident Agent

Pu m'i tua ki te ware,
E yemo miti kako okuuru tokotu.
Tairiiri toku reva kura;
Wakapaki au ko te kio;
Ye tuki-tuki te wui tane.
Tutupe toku maro wakatutu,
Uruu ma toku yana wawine.
Naku tangia na kave ki runga o te paji,
Naku tuku na tu ki te ariki—
Tuyami wakavare i raro.

From the sea to my house sounds the horn,
The topmasts are seen on the horizon's edge.
My red flag is waving;
There are cries among the spearmen;
The people are running about.
But I will wind my sennit armor about me
And hunt for my pretty young mistress.
I take her in my canoe to the great ship
And place her before the king-captain—
My mistress will soften his heart.

—*From* "Mako no te Paji" (*Chant of a visiting ship*).

XVIII

Mr. Withers—Resident Agent

IN the course of time the *Tiaré* returned, a bird-like reminder that, after all, there are other lands than Puka-Puka. Old William came to my house early one morning, grunting the ship chant. I could hardly believe him when he said that a ship was off the reef. After seven months in an empty sea, far from trade routes, without a reminder of the outside world, living among people so different from other races that they seem to belong to a planet of their own—after all these months of speaking a new language, thinking in a new groove, eating strange food, living in strange houses, under a strange code of ethics, the fact of a world beyond Danger Island had become less and less real to me. I knew, of course, that some day the schooner would return, but now that I actually saw the vessel, I found it hard to satisfy myself that its appearance was not an illusion. I was dazed, much as the early inhabitants of Puka-Puka must have been when they sighted the first ship ever to stop at the island.

I rather resented its coming, too, after the first thrill of excitement had passed, for by that time I was securely and comfortably settled in the Puka-Puka groove. Why should people from the outside world come here to disturb us, above all, ambitious, wide-awake people who never slept except at night, and who spend their lives trading utterly useless knickknacks for moldy copra that no one could possibly eat?

However, I put on my white clothes and went down to the canoe, where William awaited me. Puka-Puka was still asleep, no one but William, Mama, and I being aware that the schooner had arrived. We paddled to the reef where the *Tiaré* was already kedged, with sails furled and decks in order as though she had been there for days.

"Well, well, Ropati," said Viggo, "this is a sure sign that you've become a real Puka-Pukan. We've been here since daylight. Most traders would have been camping on the beach waiting for me."

I excused myself as best I could, explaining that no one had seen the *Tiaré* until she was kedged, but Viggo laughed away my excuses and, taking me below, had Jimmy prepare my breakfast. Viggo, never having lived on Puka-Puka, rose before daylight for his coffee instead of having it at seven in the evening.

After breakfast I gave Viggo a windy account of my trading experiences, putting in all the most minute details, thinking, Puka-Puka fashion, that they would greatly interest my friend. Viggo listened patiently, nodding his head and smiling, for he had long since learned—old, experienced trader that he is—that we hermits on lonely islands, having nothing whatever of importance to talk about, make as much as possible of the trivial events of our lonely monotonous lives. It is the same in these memoirs of mine: I know well enough how trifling they are, but I have greatly enjoyed writing them, scribbling on, thoroughly convinced that I am writing chapters of an autobiography some one will care to read. "How we apples swim!" as Dean Swift would say.

While I was in the midst of my long narration to Viggo, in stalked a gaunt, white-whiskered gentleman dressed to a T in the sort of tropical costume the mail-order houses of Sydney recommend. Viggo rose and introduced me to Mr. H. C. Withers, who, he said, was to be the government resident agent at Puka-Puka. I was rather taken aback at this but tried not to show it. Thus far we had gotten along very well at Puka-Puka without white officials, and I saw no reason for having one now.

Mr. Withers stood straight as a fence-wicket, with never a smile or a twitch of the eyebrow, and stared coldly at me for fully thirty seconds. Then he made a stiff bow and said: "Ah, Mr. Frisbie, I am gratified to know that I shall have the pleasure of the—ah—company of another white man during my sojourn on this—ah—beautiful island. I fancy that it must be rather lonely here. Are there no ladies ashore?"

"Sure!" I replied. "There's Little Sea, my wife, and her cousin Desire, and old Mama, and Sun-Eater, and Bosun-Woman and Sea Foam the preacher's wife and about two hundred others."

Just then Prendergast stuck in his head, grinning from ear to ear.

Wither's face turned boiled-lobster red, but his eyes were colder than ever and his stiff back even stiffer. "I said *ladies,* sir," he said. With that he marched out of the cabin. He was too old a man to slap, so I controlled my temper, smiling inwardly at the thought that if Little Sea and Desire were not ladies according to European standards, they were at least pretty little monkeys who made my life very pleasant and amusing.

That was my first meeting with the resident agent whom the Cook Islands administration had sent in good faith to Puka-Puka. When he was gone, Viggo said: "Now, Ropati, this is a very bad beginning for you and Mr. Withers. Two white men who are to live on such a lonely island as Puka-Puka should be friends. If you are enemies, it will be very unpleasant for both of you. Mr. Withers is not, I think, the man for such a station as this, but I believe him to be perfectly honest and I am sure that he means well. The trouble with him is that he thinks he knows how a white man should conduct himself in the tropics, never associating with the low native populations, always remembering that it is his duty to assert his superiority over the members of every other race. He considers it beneath his dignity to learn a native language or to eat native food. On the voyage up he has been very particular about what he ate, living mostly on tinned food and avoiding anything that Jimmy might have touched. I'm afraid you'll find him difficult to live with, but you really must try to be as agreeable as possible."

When I went on deck Withers was standing by the break of the poop, checking over his possessions. He eyed me icily. "Where are the coolies?" he asked.

"The what?"

"The coolies—the natives," he said peevishly.

This riled me, for I was thinking of Little Sea, Desire, old William, and the rest of my indolent, good-natured neighbors.

"Oh, the coolies," I said. "They didn't know you were coming; otherwise, of course, they would have been out long ago, shouting with joy and fighting one another to rub noses with you. Just now they are all ashore asleep. They generally sleep in the daytime. I suppose you'll change all that?"

"I certainly shall," he replied with a mirthless laugh. Then he called sharply to one of the sailors, ordering him to take his luggage ashore.

A few days later the *Tiaré* sailed, leaving the new resident agent settled in the government house near Windward Village, a good half-mile from my trading-station, thank God!

I had a fine stock of new trade goods, with plenty of Shampoo d'Or and face-powder, several cases of firecrackers, bags of marbles, all-day suckers, some pairs of shoes that squeaked beautifully, and various other supplies, together with some fish-hooks for my more sensible customers. It was early in June that for the second time I watched the *Tiaré* round the point of Leeward Village and disappear. She would not return until February of the next year—nine solitary months! Again, thank God!

For a month I saw nothing of Mr. Withers, but I heard of him through Mr. Chair and others of the amorous young fry, who came to tell me that he was trying to put an end to the love fests which he had accidentally stumbled on. Ura had been given orders which he was to transmit to Husks, Ears, and Everything, but so far there had been only a little hare-and-hounds play in the shore brush between the love-makers and the officers of the law.

Benny, too, came every now and then with news of how the resident agent had fined some one for trespassing on the government "compound" as he called it, and pigs and chickens were to be confiscated if they approached to within one hundred yards of the government "residence." Except for such official business, Mr. Withers spent his time, according to Benny, walking back and forth through the compound and in washing his clothes. His fear of contamination carried him so far that he would not even have his laundry done by a native woman, and, of course, he would eat no native food. When Sea Foam sent him a fine baked grouper and Mama presented him with a roast chicken and some baked bananas he sent them back. Not wishing to be troubled with the task of cooking, his food was all tinned stuff. The lack of fresh food soon told on him, and when, on Viggo's return, he left Puka-Puka he was in a serious condition. Still he refused to relent, and, I believe, would have starved rather than contaminate his Nordic guts with native-cooked foods. This, he believed, was the first step toward "going native"; next would come slackness in habits of personal cleanliness, leading to the native wife, and at last to the inevitable beachcomber's death.

A beachcomber's death! Well, that sort of death is often the most peaceful known to man. Many a beachcomber has eaten of the lotus, forgotten the world, loved native women, lived without malice, labor, or pain, and has died in the hope that Paradise will be like the isle he is leaving behind. The story-books often make it different, but what do the story-books know about it? Furthermore, their beachcombers are usually the hobos of the large tropical ports, such as Papeete, Apia, or Suva. Such men never reach the remote islands reserved for us epicurean beachcombers, for the reason that no South Sea skipper will consent to carry them.

On the whole, I think the stereotyped beachcomber is largely a creature of the imagination, invented by authors who write stuff about islands they have never seen. If ever they have visited the Pacific it was by steamer calling at Tahiti or Fiji, which they use as backgrounds for their yarns, built up from anecdotes overheard in the local clubs. Such are most South Sea tales. It would be as reasonable to write about Bedouin life after a hasty visit to Cairo.

I have lived for years on the loneliest islands of the eastern Pacific; I have "beachcombed" with a vengeance, abandoned myself to so-called wicked women, lived indolently, seeking pleasure wherever it was to be found, without a thought for the white man's code of ethics—and I have been happy, enjoying a felicity unknown in right-thinking realms.

To return to Mr. Withers: he had read all the story-books, and although he had been in the tropics for twenty years, no one would have guessed it. He knew nothing of native life, and was as strait-laced and narrow-minded as though he had come only yesterday from some provincial English town. Despite his thick-headed English ways, I came to like him, and before his departure he went so far as to show me the distant kind of regard one might show a person potentially of some account but who, morally, had gone to the dogs.

After his first month at Puka-Puka I visited him every Sunday afternoon. He welcomed me stiffly, without the slightest intimation that he was glad to see me, but I noticed that after I had taken an unoffered chair he would start talking eagerly, nor would he stop until I broke in with the remark that I must return to the store. At times I felt that he was almost human, and I am sure that I did him a great service by listening to his interminable harangues. I seldom had opportunity to do more than edge in a "yes" or "to be sure," but I believe that he got it into his head that I was something of a Magus Apollo, though of course an utter wreck morally.

It would bore the reader no less than myself to recount any of his long monologues and philippics against the non-British world. It is enough to say that he was forever harping upon the duty of a white man to marry a white woman, to increase the English-speaking races until they overran the world to the final extinction of all "coolies." He was a strong believer in English traditions, but he forgot to mention that many of those traditions sprang from men who flogged their slaves for the sadistic pleasure of the thing, murdered men and women in public places because they had political opinions of their own, and who tortured those who went to a different church from that of the king.

It chanced that Mr. Withers decided to visit the two other islets, Frigate Bird and Ko. In order to give an official touch to the expedition he ordered old William to rig his canoe with a comfortable chair

fixed astraddle of the gunwales. An umbrella was lashed to the back of the chair to shade His Majesty.

One breezy morning he set out with William in the stern and George and another wild youth for paddlers. Expecting disaster, George had left his overcoat at home; he came dressed only in a *pareu* and his bowler hat. The stiff figure of the resident was an odd sight, perched high in the air on a tipsy outrigger canoe. Every move he made sank the outrigger or raised it into the air, so that William had to use his utmost skill to keep the craft balanced.

This he managed for some time, when, on emerging from the bay, a gust of wind caught the umbrella and over they all went into the lagoon. All the "coolies" were on the beach; they were highly entertained.

William told me about it later, but as most of his remarks were merely profane ejaculations, the account may be greatly condensed.

"Wind come, paf! and Wibers went, pif! in the water. He try to drink all the Puka-Puka lagoon; no use, so he climbed up on the bottom of the canoe and looked at me."

"But couldn't you have prevented the canoe from upsetting?" I asked.

"Carrajo! Goddam! Of course. What you think?"

"Then why did you let it tip over?"

With true Puka-Pukan evasiveness he explained: "He made it too heavy in the top. Big umbrella; wind come, paf! Wibers go, pif! Everybody laugh but Wibers."

Mr. Withers was recalled shortly afterward and

not a trace of his influence remains. The love fests go on as before, and new broods of chickens and new litters of pigs scratch and root over the government compound. Ura, the chief of police and sometimes deacon of the church, again holds the reins of government. Ura is something of a tyrant, a sort of Puka-Pukan Porfirio Diaz, but he makes a vastly better administrator than his successor and predecessor, Mr. Withers.

XIX

An Atoll Brew

Ki inu i 'u ma te ramu—
Ye aku mua te ute,
Upaupa au pe te neneva,
Akalongolongo atu i 'u
Na rek'i au e to reo,
Wi ake 'i aku akan'u—
Ki inu i 'u ma te ramu.

I will drink rum,
I will sing songs
And dance like a man possessed.
I will listen to the merry-making
While I dance,
Beating my thighs together.
I will drink rum.

—*From* "Mako Ono-ono" (*a Puka-Puka drinking song*).

XIX

An Atoll Brew

AT the time of Viggo's first return to Puka-Puka, while rummaging among the ship's stores for some delicacies to take ashore, I discovered a considerable stock of malt extracts and hops, some packages of raisins, and several jars of maple syrup. Not being altogether an ignoramus in the fine art of brewing, I took all of these articles that Viggo could spare. As a brewing receptacle was then required, Viggo, with his usual ability to furnish almost anything needed in the islands, sent ashore an old crockery water-cooler of eight gallons' content, and a five-gallon demijohn.

For many months thereafter I experimented in home brews, and the more I concocted, the more convinced I became that the simpler the brew the better. I finally adopted the following recipe:

¾ pound of hops boiled in seven gallons of water
5 pounds of washed rice
6 pounds of brown sugar
1¼ pounds of malt extract
1 tablespoon of salt.

When the hops water has cooled, it is strained into the eight-gallon crock and the other ingredients added. When making the first brew it is a good plan to add a little yeast, but this is not important except in cold weather. When the brewing has entirely ceased and all the sediment has precipitated, leaving a clear fluid with a moldy scum on top, the ale is dipped out carefully so as not to stir up the sediment, and strained into another receptacle, where a half pound of sugar is added. Then it is bottled, preferably in crown-cap bottles, for if others are used great care must be taken in fastening down the corks.

One soon learns that the less sediment, the better the brew. When I wish a specially fine brew I pour the ale directly from the barrel into a demijohn, allow it to stand for about a week until a perfectly clear fluid is obtained, then drain it carefully into another receptacle, add the sugar—a half pound to eight gallons—and bottle.

In making the second brew the same rice is used over again, with an additional half-pound of new rice.

In fact, the rice should never be thrown away, for the longer it is used, the better the ale. In the first brews it imparts a slightly raw taste, but in the fourth or fifth brews this disappears and one has a perfect beverage. In making my brews I wash the rice after every other brew, so as to eliminate a part of the sediment. There is, however, a diversity of opinion on this matter among contemporary atoll brewers. One gifted artist at Rarotonga never washes his old rice, while another, on the island of Mangaia, washes his thoroughly after every brew. The Rarotonga artist's ale has a fine flavor but is somewhat cloudy; and while the Mangaia brewer's ale is as clear as the fountain of Arethusa, it often has a raw taste due to the necessity of adding at least a pound of new rice to each brew to make up for the coarse sediment and broken rice lost in the process of washing. Therefore, I adhere to my middle course of washing the rice after every other brew.

Of course, one is greatly tempted to consume the brew during the first week or two after it is finished, but one should exert the utmost self-restraint and leave it for six weeks, when it is at its prime in this climate (probably a longer time is needed in cooler latitudes). At the end of this time he will have six brews of forty bottles each, that is, provided he brews steadily. He may then enjoy forty bottles of mature ale each week, which is just enough to keep one in good health. In my own case, I keep two or three brews going at once so that I have from eighty to one hundred and twenty bottles a week—none too generous a supply, for I find that I have more friends now than I did during the earlier dry season.

I used the raisins and maple syrup for wine. It is made as follows: Crush five pounds of raisins and pour them into a five-gallon demijohn; add three pounds of washed rice, six of brown sugar, and one pound of maple syrup or honey. Then fill the demijohn with water that has been boiled and allowed to cool. If hot water is poured in, the wine will not ferment. Fermentation is completed in from twenty-five to thirty days, depending on the temperature. During this time the demijohn is closed with three thicknesses of calico tied over the mouth. When fermentation has stopped, the wine is bottled and corked lightly. At the end of a week or two it is carefully decanted into new bottles. Thus clear wine is obtained. It is now corked tightly and the bottles are stored, lying on their sides, for at least three months. A year is better, and some of my wine, now three or four years old, is really excellent. But new raisin wine is nauseating stuff, with a vinegary flavor and ruinous to the digestion.

For some time before my first brew was ready I had been suffering from digestive complaints, malnutrition, and general debility, due to the enervating nature of the climate. A so-called perfect climate, like that of Puka-Puka, where the temperature never drops below 70 nor rises above 85, often proves injurious to one's general health. Without cooler weather one's system becomes sluggish and unable to resist disorders that would hardly be noticed in a more severe climate.

But when my first brew was six weeks old, Benny and I made it a daily habit to empty five or six bottles, whereupon I quickly recovered my health, could eat anything and digest it, too, and found my system generally toned up in a remarkable degree.

As my ale became known on the island, the Puka-Pukans began to develop various internal complaints for which my home-brew was the only possible remedy. They would appear at the trading-station at 8 P.M. sharp with such regularity and precision that I could set the store clock by their appearance. They made their headquarters in the back room of the station, where the bottles were stored. My most regular visitors were Ura, chief of police; Husks, the policeman from Central Village; Benny, and Pain-in-the-Head (Upoku-Mamao), an Aitutaki native who had been captivated by Puka-Puka indolence and one of the island maidens. Sometimes Wail-of-Woe's father, Breadfruit, dragged his elephantiasis legs into the back room to partake of a few glasses to relieve the filarial fever; and often dear old rheumy-eyed Bones came in with his pig and his mouth organ to sit cross-legged, fondly gazing at the store of bottled refreshment stacked along the wall. Despite his depravity, I have a sort of liking for old Bones, and I could always get rid of him by saying that I had just seen a bevy of damsels making their way to the lonely outer beach.

After a few months of brewing it occurred to me that since I now had "jolly good ale and old," and excellent wine too, I might as well have a bar to drink it over. So I laid a couple of boards across two boxes and built some shelves, the back of which I decorated with corked empty bottles: Black and White, Dubonnet, Peach Brandy, Crême de Menthe, St. James Rum, etc., as well as a few tins of Vienna sausage and Rex cheese. A bottle of pickles, cigars, some tins of cigarettes and some cartons of safety matches completed the picture. Then I made a conspicuous sign, marked:

LINE ISLANDS TRADING COMPANY
BAR

and hung it from a rafter. Then I stepped behind the bar and said to the imaginary customer on the other side: "What'll it be, sir, beer? Puka-Puka Prize Ale?" whereupon I stepped round to the other side and said, "Yes; not too much head on it, please," and, in lieu of a nickel, threw a sixpence on the counter. The first glass of ale ever served across a bar in the history of Puka-Puka was deliciously refreshing, and the bartender, with old-time American hospitality, served me with a tasty snack to enjoy with the beer: sausage, bread, and pickles. Afterward I smoked a cigar and offered one to the bartender, which he accepted and put in his waistcoat pocket.

At 8 P.M. Benny, Ura, Husks, and Pain-in-the-Head awoke and came in for eye-openers. I put the chief of police behind the bar, instructed him in his duties, and we four convivial spirits sprawled along the counter drinking ale and telling yarns till cockcrow. It was that morning, I remember, that I started three brews going instead of one.

XX

Gamblers All

Pat'it'i i te m'itaki i te pirara n'i
Ya pata-pati i te orire.
Eje m'ua m'i i te m'itaki
Kia kii te pute i te pata.
Kua ka kore toku ngutuare
Na pat'it'i i te pirara.
Manako koe ka ngere 'u?
T'ie te apinga makeke tu!

The Troublemaker wastes my substance
Playing marbles in the village;
No wealth she brings me
To fill my pockets.
Because of the Troublemaker's losses
My house is empty.
But you think I have nothing left?
Behold my straight rod!

—*From* "Mako no te Paré" (*Puka-Puka gambler's lament*).

XX

Gamblers All

ONE Saturday afternoon I dropped in for a chat with Sea Foam and found him scribbling on a slate the notes for the morrow's sermon.

"You see, Ropati," he said in the course of our conversation, "I don't mind the children playing marbles, even though they do play hookey from school, for there are always plenty of children at school anyway. The trouble is with the fathers and mothers: they gamble in their marble games. Ura, who is just now one of our church deacons, is among the worst offenders. It is sinful!

"Only yesterday," the good parson went on, "I found my wife, Bones, and Ezekiel playing marbles behind the school-house, and the worst of it was that they had cheated my wife out of every one of her marbles. Now she will be pestering me for some of my own marbles that I have saved and stored away in the bottom of my camphor-wood chest with the musical lock."

I suggested to Sea Foam that I might, perhaps, divert the people's interest from marbles by starting some other game, checkers, for example, or top-spinning, or cat's-cradle (*waivai*), or perhaps kite-flying, for I had observed that none of the men had been flying kites for months. All that was needed was for some one to start a new craze. Sea Foam agreed with this and asked me to do what I could in this way to put a stop to the marble-playing.

The following Monday there was a great church festival and all the people were gathered in the churchyard. Various competitive games were in progress: spear-throwing, dancing (males only), coconut-husking, and the like. Then came a food-eating contest.

For this competition each of the villages chose their champions, with an eye to their height and girth rather than for speed in eating. Fat sea-birds had been roasted in great numbers, and the three champions, well starved beforehand so as to make them particularly ravenous, started in on them, crunching them bones and all, while the spectators bet wildly on the result. It was an incredible gorging-bee; the contestants were well matched, and for a long time the outcome hung in the balance. At last two of them fell over with bloated groans and were carried off the field, leaving the winner still able to chew but not to swallow. Every one yelled with delight and the children scrambled for the remains of the feast.

I watched the festivities for a while; many marble games were going here and there, and it occurred to me that this was a favorable opportunity for starting the new game I had promised Sea Foam. So I collected old William, Bones, George, Abraham, King-of-the-Sky, Pain-in-the-Head, and a few others, and led them behind the church, where I produced a pair of ivory cubes marked with strange geometric dots, and initiated them into the now all but lost art of rolling the bones. My novices were keenly interested and in a very few moments they understood perfectly all the points of the game. I said nothing to them about gambling, knowing that nothing need be said. Puka-Pukans are like the Chinese in their love for games of chance.

When I returned, half an hour later, Bones, King-of-the-Sky, and the rest were squatting back of the church, each with a great heap of coconuts beside him, as much wealth of this sort as they could amass at short notice. It was odd to hear their cries as they rolled the dice: they had found immediately perfect Puka-Pukan equivalents for the American "Little Joe!" "Come Seven! Baby needs a new pair of shoes!" etc.

The natives at the festival on the other side of the church soon got wind of the fact that something unusual was happening. Not infrequently a head would be poked round the corner, and soon the rest of the body would follow. After looking on for a few moments, the new-comer would sneak home for a sack of his wife's husked coconuts and presently would be shooting a profoundly studied game.

By midday the wide space of sun-bleached coral in

front of the church was all but deserted. Spears had been left lying where they fell among the larger bones of sea-birds, and of the great piles of coconuts used in the husking competitions nothing was left but the husks themselves. Sea Foam sat in his steamer chair beneath a huge red umbrella abandoned by all his flock. He beckoned to me as I was returning home.

"Ropati," he said, blinking gravely at me, "what is this new game you've started?"

I began, apologetically, to explain, while Sea Foam listened with interest.

"I think I'd better see it," he said, rising with an effort and adjusting his bandmaster cap.

A great crowd was gathered behind the church, and in the midst of it was Mrs. Sea Foam rolling the bones as though she had been playing African golf for years. She had a huge pile of winnings behind her, and as we pushed our way through the crowd we heard her shout: *"Iaau! Lautai! Hau mai te akaari!"* which may be almost precisely translated: "Wow! Eleven! Give me the coconuts!"

Sea Foam looked on in silence for a few minutes, but I noticed that his eyes sparkled more and more brightly as his wife added to her gains.

"Ropati," he said, "what is it you call this game?"

Before the afternoon was over, Sea Foam had amassed a pile of seven hundred coconuts, most of which he won from old William the heathen. From that time on marbles were forgotten.

Despite his losses to Sea Foam, William soon became one of the wealthiest men on the island. Frequently he brought me four or five bags of copra which he had won in a single evening. My one pair of dice would not suffice, of course, for the crap-shooters of three villages, so dice were made from bits of a hard white coral found in the lagoon, which they ground down, shaped, polished, and marked in beautiful fashion.

The old men were the privileged rollers of the bones; the younger men looked on, making side bets on their favorite players. On the outer reef there was a great slab of coral, perfectly smooth, where the old and qualified experts played in the midst of a crowd watching in hushed and breathless silence. For a time Sea Foam played constantly, but at last, having lost heavily, his conscience began to trouble him and he preached a fiery sermon against gambling. He tried to enlist Ura on his side, and the chief of police went so far as to have an ordinance passed prohibiting crap-shooting before 4 P.M. This prohibition really came as a relief to everybody, for too long had the Puka-Pukans been deprived of their day-long siestas. Now they could sleep in peace till the evening without missing any of the big games, which henceforth started at four and proceeded, by torchlight, until far into the night.

II

Marble-playing and crap-shooting are by no means the only games of chance indulged in at Puka-Puka, and in addition to games, properly speaking, the natives have other methods of giving vent to their sporting instincts. One of the most singular of these is their fish-gambling.

One afternoon I was sitting on my back veranda overlooking the lagoon, idly watching George, who was putting his canoe in the water. He was about to push off when old Mama, greatly excited, hobbled out, waving her arms and calling to him to wait a moment. When she reached him she said: "I'll bet a hundred coconuts you don't catch a jewfish!"

George bet two hundred he would catch three. Mama was game and raised him another hundred, and the final wager was a thousand nuts. All of this required a great deal of excited talk, during which a crowd gathered and the gambling started in earnest. The fisherman's friends and relatives wagered that he would catch his three, while others, listening to Mama, who swore that she had a "hunch," betted on her side. Soon most of the island's portable property was in the scales, and Ura, Ears, Husks, and Everything were called upon to witness the bets.

George went home to get his army overcoat, for the function was assuming a semi-public nature and it would never do for him to appear on such an occasion dressed in a grass skirt. After buttoning up his great trench-coat he pushed his canoe out into the lagoon and, in the midst of shouts of advice and encouragement from his supporters, paddled to a coral mushroom near the reef and started his memorable jewfishing.

At first he had no luck. Every known variety of fish bit except the one he wanted. But at the end of several hours he caught one jewfish. He waved it aloft, while his backers cheered exultantly.

Night came, and morning, and another night, and George fished doggedly on. On the second morning he waved another jewfish, but only one. The day became exceptionally warm and at last he was obliged to take off his overcoat. Many of the villagers expected him to give up that night. They betted on it. The excitement was intense.

For two days practically no one slept. Now and then some one would lie down under a tree for a few hours of feverish sleep, but otherwise the vigil was unbroken. Men forgot everything but the gamble.

The third morning saw the end of it. The population of the three villages had spent the night on the beach, and when dawn broke they saw George paddling dejectedly ashore. He had caught but two jewfish. Great were the rejoicings of old Mama and her faction. I have never seen George, the dandy, so crestfallen as he was on this occasion.

XXI

Infidelity

E toa tikai 'u!
Naku turekina turuaki,
Na yinga ki raro!
Naku welia te nga roto,
Na moe ki raro!
Na yiyila 'u ki te potiki,
Ya rere rua te koji-manava!
E toa tikai 'u!

I am a warrior!
Easily I won the first-born
One moonlight night in the love fests.
The second one was also conquered
Through my tempestuous advances.
The youngest, too, I was not slow
To favor with my affections.
I am a warrior!

—*From* "Mako no te Akaturi" (*love chant of a Puka-Puka Don Juan*).

Infidelity

AFTER solitary years on a remote island one arrives at a curious state of mind. One becomes lost at times in a world of one's own, blind to passing events, deaf to the monotonous clamor of children, unconscious of heat, cold, wind, sunlight, or shadow. One lives in a "mind world," so to speak, which is quite indescribable to normal persons, because the images which exist there and the events which happen there are not evoked by words, either spoken or thought. Strange as it may seem, one thinks without words.

I had often tried to picture imaginary events without uttering, mentally, so much as a syllable, but for long I found it impossible, and many people, I know, believe that it must always be impossible. They hold that without words as mediums it is quite impossible to think at all. I do not agree with them. I have learned, through constant practice, how to do this, how to detach myself from the world where words are necessary to evoke images, and to enter a kingdom of my own. But I had best not attempt to describe this kingdom lest the reader think me quite mad, which I hope I am not.

Sleeping open-eyed is a different matter, although the faculty for doing so is, perhaps, allied to that for thinking without words, as animals think—if they may be said to think. I can do that too, now; it is one of those curious accomplishments one is bound to acquire at such a place as Puka-Puka. All the natives have it. They sink into trances with perfect ease, sitting bolt upright, their eyes open, completely unconscious of the world about them.

I recall vividly the night when I was first able to do so. I was sitting on my front balcony, chewing the husks of a sweet variety of coconut called *mangaro*. Little Sea had eaten her fill and had leaned back to fall into the untroubled sleep of the young savage. I fell to thinking, for some strange reason, of her cousin Desire, who was again living with her mother, having left us about three months before because Little Sea thought I was becoming too greatly interested in her.

Abraham, George's father, was sitting in front of an adjacent house, the light of a fire throwing his figure into clear relief against the wattled wall at his back. He sat cross-legged, his arms hanging limply at his side, the backs of his hands resting on the ground. He was staring vacantly straight in front of him, and I knew that he was in one of the trances so common to Puka-Pukans. I called out his name, but he stared on, as completely unconscious of his surroundings as though he had been in the deepest sleep. I have often asked the natives what they think of at such times, and they invariably reply: "Of nothing." They say it is just like a dreamless sleep, only when they are really asleep they are more easily wakened.

I turned my eyes from Abraham and leaned back in my steamer chair. Then I heard some one passing below, I rose, looked over the veranda railing, and saw little Desire in a red and white *pareu* and a wreath of gardenias on her pretty head. She was strolling . . . where, I wondered . . . to the love fests?

A surge of passion rose in me. Desire was in the first bloom of womanhood, slim, graceful, with a seductive, tantalizing mouth, the lips just full enough to be warmly passionate. Leaning over the railing I called to her.

She stopped to glance up with an alluring smile, her head up-tilted, the moonlight falling softly on her smooth shoulders.

What could be more beautiful than olive skin in the moonlight? Before I realized what I was doing I had slipped down and had her in my arms.

It must have been after midnight when I returned to the veranda. Little Sea was still asleep, her head pillowed on her arm. I felt a twinge of remorse, which was more than most South Sea traders would have felt under like circumstances.

"Why in the world," I thought, "should I be making love to Desire when I have such a really lovable wife? I'll do it no more, that's certain!"

The words sounded very brave, but somehow they failed to quench the fire within me. I sat down again in my steamer chair, determined to banish the thoughts of Desire from my mind, and after a considerable effort I succeeded. Hazy thoughts and hazy visions drifted across consciousness, becoming less and less distinct until I became oblivious of my surroundings, of my identity, of existence itself.

Of a sudden I awoke. Little Sea was shaking me by the shoulder.

"Ropati!" she said, "you are as bad as old Abraham: you fall asleep with your eyes open!"

I was sitting precisely as I had been when I went into the trance, and my eyes were, in truth, wide open. I felt as completely refreshed as though I had had a sound night's sleep, and it was then only about three in the morning. But the villages were more widely awake at that hour than they would be at dawn. Fires glimmered through the groves; fishermen were coming in from their lobster-spearing along the reef, and a sing-song, or *himené,* was going at full tilt in Leeward Village.

As I rose to enter the house I saw old Abraham still sitting open-eyed, by his doorway like a Puka-Pukan Buddha. His old wife was broiling a lobster directly in front of him, the night life of Puka-Puka was going blithely forward, and he no more aware of it than I had been a few moments before. I called down to ask the old lady how long he had been sitting there and she replied "All night." A moment later she shook him vigorously, both hands on his shoulders.

The old man was sufficiently roused at length, and moved up to the fire to join his family in their three-o'clock-in-the-morning supper.

Little Sea found out immediately, of course, that I had been carrying-on with Desire. The next morning when she brought me my coffee she set down the cup with a little toss of her head.

"Hmph!" she said. "I was right, after all. Well, I'm glad that you picked my cousin instead of some strange woman."

XXII

William Discusses Women

Toriia te mea mata nga reka,
Te mea moto mata kati-kati;
Ruaki raro ke p'u ake,
M'i te koua e tae uatu ki te taka-taka.

Run, bring me a drinking-nut,
And one still younger;
Bring nuts here for me to eat,
From the green baby nut to the brown ripe grandmother.

—*From* "Mako Ono-ono" (*a Puka-Puka love chant*).

William Discusses Women

ONE evening, shortly after the adventure related in the last chapter, I was walking through the groves thinking about Desire. I had about made up my mind to have nothing more to do with her: it appealed to my pride to make a gesture of abnegation and be true to Little Sea; furthermore, for all the fact that I had lived for so many years in the South Sea, vestiges of my northern birth and training still remained with me. I found it difficult to convince myself that, whatever the relations might become between Desire and me, they could not injure Little Sea in the least.

Observing a coconut-palm growing at an easily scalable angle, I decided to climb it to catch the breeze while I smoked my evening pipe. Upon reaching the top, whom should I find there but my old friend William perched on a cluster of nuts jammed between a frond-butt and the tree. He was leaning comfortably back in a mass of foliage, sucking an empty pipe. I

offered him my pouch, which he gravely accepted, filled his pipe, and motioned me to a perch on a neighboring bunch of nuts.

Having made myself comfortable, I lit my own pipe and leaned back to enjoy a quiet smoke while the wind swayed the tree gently, with a pleasant cradlelike motion.

Old William livened up at my arrival. Producing a six-foot piece of string, he tied the ends together and, after looping it around the index and little fingers of each hand, proceeded by rapid manipulations to form complex patterns in the string between his fingers. School-girls in America often amuse themselves in this way, making what they call "cat's-cradles," but their patterns are simplicity itself in comparison with old William's.

The Puka-Puka string figures are of very ancient origin. Local legends tell how the gods of Puka-Puka taught them to the people. One legend relates how the famous Polynesian god, the oldest Maui (Maui-matua), visited Puka-Puka and challenged the people to test his wisdom. The local heroes and gods started making string patterns before him, asking what they represented. Each pattern he named correctly: "This is *Po-nao-nao;* this is the oven of *Lau-tara;* this is *Tii-koni-koni,*" etc. But one hero made a puzzle which Maui was to unravel. The god tried and failed. In order to save his honor he directed the attention of the local hero to a large bird in an adjacent tree, and while the hero was looking away Maui undid the puzzle by breaking the string, much as Alexander cut the Gordian knot.

Heathen William, like the rest of the inhabitants, had made a life study of string patterns. His skill was really marvelous. The old man's bony fingers were almost invisible as he manipulated the string; then he would stop abruptly, spread his hands, and show me a new design. Throughout the performance his coarse old face was wrinkled with a self-satisfied smile.

"This is a shark," he would say, showing me a new pattern, and he would grunt a song specially composed for that particular picture; "this is a flock of birds over a school of fish; this is Ko Islet after a great hurricane." Many of his patterns were of such a nature that they could hardly have been shown at a Ladies' Sewing Circle; as for his explanations of their meaning, it is enough to say that they are what one would expect from old Danger Island William.

"Now," he said, "I will show you one of the most difficult of all. Not many people can make this one." His fingers moved so rapidly that it was impossible to follow their movements, and the string was crossed and recrossed so many times that at last there was a space of only a few inches between his hands. He stopped, spread his fingers, and exhibited the pattern. "What would you call that?" he asked, grinning at me.

I shook my head.

"Carramba! What-ta-hell! Don't you know what that is? What they teach you in the white man's school? It's a cowboy having a great battle on the outside beach at night." He rolled his eyes and wiggled his thumbs, whereupon the complicated tangle worked back and forth in an indescribable manner. Old William roared with laughter and nearly fell out of the tree in his merriment. Then he put the string back in his pocket, saying that he would show me some more patterns at another time.

I shifted to a softer cluster of nuts and relit my pipe, which had gone out in the thick of William's graphic battle. We were silent for some time. At length I said, "William, what is your greatest pleasure in life?"

Without a moment's hesitation the sage of Puka-Puka replied: "Shooting marbles; that is, nowadays.

But when I was a wild youth I was a terror with the women. Now I am a worthless old lubber and no one but a *koari* will even look at me!"

"A *koari?*" I said. "What's that?"

He explained that a *koari* is a green undeveloped coconut that has fallen from a tree due to the depredations of wind, rats, or small boys. The nut shrivels like an old woman, becoming practically worthless.

"In these days," he went on, "the Puka-Puka youth are as foolish as the white men, for they listen to the teachings of the missionaries and try to ape the white men's ways. Now when a young Puka-Puka man wants a wife he asks her father's permission to marry, and he wastes his money buying her worthless trinkets from the trading schooners: dresses and shoes and *pareus* and the like, when it would be much better to spend his money on himself, buying all-day suckers, tops, marbles, or Japanese kites. In the end he often marries the girl without having known her more than a month or two in the love fests. Blood and damnation! Unless you live with a wench a few years, how are you going to know what she is? More than likely you'll find that she won't do any work at all, and then what compensation have you got for your loss of freedom?"

William expressed his opinion of such modern practice in a singeing blast of curses. He spat venomously over the side of the tree and proceeded to tell me how different things had been when he was young. Those were the good old times when real men lived. When he wanted a wife, as was often the case, he chose her without asking her father, her mother, or even herself. He simply took her, whether she liked it or not. He had learned early in life that all women like masterful men.

The old heathen chuckled to himself as he thought of past days. "Ah, when I was a youth," he resumed presently, "women were nice and fat."

"It seems to me, William," I said, "although of course I am no fit judge, being only a white trader, that a fat woman is not a desirable mate."

"Why?" he asked, surprised. "Carramba! They are a lot better than the *koaris,* the skinny ones."

"Well," I said, "my wife, Little Sea, whom you have admitted to be a fine girl, is slender."

"Haw, haw, haw!" roared the old heathen. "Why, she's nothing but a *koua!*"

A *koua* is a young budding coconut about the size of a golf-ball.

"Of course," he went on, "she'll fill out in time to a nice fat *uivaka;* then she'll become a *niumata katikati;* after that she'll be a *niumata,* and after that a *niumatua,* and by and by she'll be waddling around your house, a nice filled up *niukatea.*" He described all the stages in the development of the coconut, and ended by saying: "Bleed me! and when all's finished and she's turned out nice and brown, with plenty of meat on her, she'll be just like a fine round *akaari*" (a mature coconut).

Somewhat awed by this display of island erudition, I said: "But can't you find a more suitable way of describing Puka-Puka women than by comparing them to the various stages in the growth of a coconut?"

"No," said William, "there's nothing equal to a coconut for describing women from childhood to old age. We can hoist them skys'l high when we say they are like a *koari*. Bones and blood! And when a woman grows old and hard we say: 'Oh, all right, she's a good-enough *taka-taka!*' You savee the *taka-taka?* It's an old coconut that's got no juice inside and the meat dried to a fine brown color, like copra.

"*Aué!* Hell's pickles! But I'm an old lubber now and not even a *koari* cares anything about old William any more! Vamose! Finish! Anyhow, I get some pleasure playing marbles in my old age."

"But look at old Bones," I said. "He's as old as you are, William, but he's still a great hand with the women."

"That old fool!" said William, snorting scornfully. "But he plays the mouth organ; and when the fine fat *niukateas* hear him they think he's a young man again!"

The sun was just setting, but William and I, having refilled our pipes, had no intention of leaving our comfortable perch. A wayward hen, too proud to roost with the other hens on the village church, had come to our coconut-palm and was *cluck-clucking* petulantly, for half-way up the tree she had spied us occupying her roost. The breeze had died away and the tree was now quite motionless save when William's statements required forcible gesticulations, which made it sway in a gentle nodding manner as though it were confirming every word the old sage uttered.

"Speaking of women," he went on, "have you heard the death chant I am making for old Mama?"

"What!" I said, "do you mean to say you are composing a death chant for old Mama?"

"Carramba! Yes! Why not? She's an old woman; she won't last many more moons."

Then in his wheezy guttural voice he began chanting a song beginning:

Akaru na ke, akat'ia,
Opotia ki te konga et'i,
Ru na niwan'unga vavare . . .

I shall gather them all in one place,
My wife and her three sisters,
For they have all been kind to old William . . .

I remarked that I thought it was a shame to compose a death chant for his wife when she was still in her usual health, and furthermore, to brag about his past love affairs with his wife's sisters. "You don't know the Bible, William, because you are an old heathen; but there it says: 'Neither shalt thou take a wife to her sister, to vex her, . . . beside the other, in her life time.' "

"The Bible! I don't want to know anything about that foolishness! If it says that it's wrong to make love to your wife's sisters, then it's even more foolish than I thought. Your wife is glad when you take a fancy to her sisters. She knows then that you're not making love to some other woman's sisters."

"Then you think it's natural for a man to make love to more than one woman?"

"Of course! What you think? You think any man makes love to only one woman? No Puka-Puka woman believe that, or Puka-Puka man either—not when they're young. But listen to the rest of my song."

He chanted away for at least twenty minutes, speaking now and then of poor old Mama, but for the most part exalting himself, speaking of his whaling days, of his liaisons with women of other islands, and giving a list of the names of those he had at various times honored with his affections.

I confess that I was rather shocked at William's callousness, at the thought that he was so little concerned over the prospect of old Mama's death that he could compose a long, and certainly lewd, song in her, or rather in his own, honor. I wondered what would happen if I were to die on Puka-Puka. The natives would have a big time, unquestionably. They would compose a death chant—Bosun-Woman would very likely be given the job of composing it; Little Sea and Desire would wail piteously over my body for a day, and then I should be quickly forgotten.

And what was I, after all, but a somewhat more highly sensitized Mama? She was an old savage who gesticulated furiously, wore a grass skirt much too thin, and had the most absurd notions about the world beyond Puka-Puka. When she died it would be merely the dissolving into Nirvana of various illusions about steamboats, foreign lands, and the ways to make taro pudding. As for myself, it would be much the same thing, except that illusions would be a trifle more concrete, and those concerned with taro pudding replaced by others concerning the best method of making home-brew. William interrupted my musing. "Here's the ending of the song," he said. But the ending, I am afraid, was rather too broad to be translated here.

Dusk had deepened as we sat there, and people were waking from their all-day slumbers. William, apparently, had only just begun to talk. He proposed that he should give me the complete history of his life; but I was cramped from sitting so long in the same position, so we slid down the tree and returned to the village.

XXIII

The Sea Afire

Taku tae akamau i tua
Tu wuri Tioti te toa maroro,
Na toa 'u no te pereue n'i,
Na tari o te kainga n'i.
Tere te witi-witi, te kapu-kapu,
Yaea ki te tae kau roroa.

E mate no Ngake ma Yato
Ko te puta i te maroro.
Koa worerua mai te moana,
Koa yayakina te marae—
Ko Tioti te angai i te w'i tangata.

When I go to sea,
I, George, the champion netter,
I, the champion of the army coat,
All the people follow me.
The fish, great and small, fly from me.

I conquer the Leeward and Windward Villagers
In catching the flying-fish.
All know of me, from the creatures in the sea
To the spirits in the burial grounds.
I am George who feeds the villages.

—*From* "Mako Wahinganga no Tihoti" (*George's flying-fish chant*).

The Sea Afire

"O YEZ! It's like this," George shouted one night as he stood in the road below, clad in his great army coat, and posed in an attitude of great self-importance. He was acting, for the moment, as town-crier. I raised my head to glance from the veranda.

"I, George, being the principal man of Leeward Village, have taken it upon myself to challenge all the world to go flying-fish netting to-morrow night. The rest of Leeward Village will assist me. There will be ten canoes to a village, three men in each canoe—two men with nets and a third with torches. Each man will bring three torches so there will be nine to a canoe."

He then spoke in the usual boastful manner of his progenitors, added a flaming panegyric upon himself, and strolled down the road to repeat his speech at the next house.

The following night at about eight o'clock, Benny,

my store-boy, Husks, the Roto policeman, and I set out in a canoe to join the competition. Benny was forward, for he is an expert with a net, and that position is most important. Husks was in the stern, also with a net, while I occupied the center with nine long torches lying on the outrigger supports beside me. Each torch was made of two dry coconut fronds lashed into a tight bundle. The nets were similar to a landing-net, except that they were secured to light ten-foot poles so that they could be thrust out a good distance to sweep up the fish.

We crossed the reef at the leeward side of the islet and formed in single file, parallel to the reef and about fifty yards from it, facing south. George came last, as is the custom with the challenger. After we

had crossed the reef he lit one of his torches, and as the two men in his canoe paddled the length of the line he held out his torch to light those in each of the remaining twenty-nine canoes. Then he took his place at the head of the line, while we all held our torches close to the sea, where they smoldered. Sometimes, when they flared up, we sprinkled a little water on them, for we did not wish to frighten away the fish.

At a signal from George we made a flank movement which brought our canoes facing the reef. Then George's torch-bearer raised his torch to a perpendicular position, where it immediately burst into flames. George and the man in the stern of his canoe instantly jumped on the gunwales, nets in hand. Then

the second canoe's torch was raised, and the third, the fourth, and so on, until in the course of half a minute the sea was alight with the reflections of thirty great frond flambeaux, blazing so brightly that one could have seen to read by their light a quarter of a mile away.

What a mad scene followed! The air was alive with panic-stricken fish whizzing past us, sometimes thudding against our bodies or the sides of the canoes. Others zigzagged madly along the surface, dashing blindly here and there in an effort to get into the open sea. Nets flew out in a flash, handled by the men standing upright on the gunwales of each canoe as they balanced themselves in a truly marvelous manner on their precarious perches. They dashed their nets into the water, or thrust them out in the air unerringly, to catch fish on the wing; and when one was in the net it was cast into the canoe with a swift backward sweep. There was no time to waste in picking him out of the net, for in a minute the fish would be gone. I often expected to see the fish fall into the sea instead of the canoe, but they always landed safely, to expire with a final flop.

Husks grunted each time he thrust out his net, much as an old man grunts when chopping wood. Benny, growing a trifle fat on good feeding and daily beer at the trading-station, chanted wildly as he performed wonders at balancing and netting. Sleek-limbed, oily-skinned, healthy as a shark, and quick as a dolphin, his net flew so fast that it dizzied me to watch him. In two minutes he must have caught twenty fish.

What an adventure that torch-fishing was to me!

Because of the blinding light we could not see the land nor the lagoon; but the reef loomed up, monstrous, fantastic, spouting spray and foam; and each undulation of the sea was augmented by the shadows cast by the torchlight, much as the bumps and hollows in a road are magnified in the motorist's eyes by the shadows caused by his headlights. The great swells thundered on the reef and the backwash poured down over the brink to make a choppy sea, with small waves like dolphins raising their heads to stare at us. The torch-light threw a ruddy glare on the bronze skins of the fishermen, naked save for the red strips of cloth about their loins—ninety yelling, singing, grunting savages in the midst of thousands of panic-stricken fish. Above was appalling blackness, which hung just over our heads, held off by the blazing light of the torches but ready to engulf us when the last ember had died away.

In and out of the line moved a dozen small one-man canoes occupied by such octogenarians as old William, Bones, and Abraham. They were trolling for the jacks feeding on the flying-fish. The old men would catch five or six each in the course of the evening, a delicacy far more palatable than flying-fish, which are tasty only when quite fresh. Later I often joined the old men, preferring a few fat jacks and the less strenuous method of fishing. But I think the old men always resented having a young buck like myself joining their privileged band.

After three or four minutes the flying-fish were either captured or had escaped. George lowered his torch, a sign for us to do likewise, and we paddled slowly along the reef until we were in new water. I noticed that one canoe had fallen out of line and was passing us rapidly, the men digging their paddles into the water with the hollow singing sound that only a Puka-Puka paddle will make. Benny explained that it is customary for the last canoe in line to take the lead after the first fishing and so on until each canoe has had its turn at leading. This is done because the men in the first canoe are in a position to catch more fish than the others, so all are given an equal chance. After the first netting, most of the fish are near the leading canoe, it being farthest from the fished water. For that reason the leading canoe raises its torch first, then one by one in regular succession the others are flashed out, driving the flying-fish down the line so that all the canoes will have a chance at them, although the ones near the head of the line have the advantage. As for the fish, they have but little chance, for they are blocked on one side by the reef and on the other by the canoes, while the two open ends are too narrow to be discovered.

After each of the thirty canoes had led, our supply of torches was exhausted, and one by one we left the line and paddled back to the shallow passage over the reef. It must have been after eleven when Benny, Husks, and I grounded our canoe on the beach back of the trading-station. We had more than two hundred fish, and Little Sea and Desire met us with the usual squeals of delight, for they were hungrily looking forward to a big feast.

When all the canoes had returned, the fish were taken to the churchyard, where Sea Foam counted them and wrote the names of the men, the village, and the number in each catch in the fly-leaf of a Bible. It was found that George has been as good as his boast, his canoe having netted no less than three hundred and eighty fish. Ears came second with three hundred and twelve. All together, we caught five thousand four hundred and some odd, Leeward Village having totaled the most. This entitled that village to a song and dance, and the usual comedy took place, George leading Mr. Chair's society in a wild midnight dance descriptive of the great prowess of Leeward Village and the utter worthlessness of the inhabitants of the two other settlements. On dividing the fish, each man, woman, and child received ten, and the remaining hundred or so were added to Sea Foam's share, as the custom is.

Desire and Little Sea lit a fire of coconut shells on a clean patch of gravel behind the store, and when the flames had died down they laid the fish on the odorless coals, head, scales and all, and we inhaled the rich aroma of broiling flesh. When the fish were ready we split some coconuts, I produced a few bottles of beer, Benny appeared from nowhere, as he always does when there is something to drink, and we made a party of it. On unrolling the fish from their skins, dainty white flesh was laid open, which is delicious when eaten with coconut. Such a feast, with a few glasses of my own inimitable home-brew to wash it down, is perfect.

XXIV

Tata and Toto

Kua topa Tata ma Toto i te moana,
Na wapuka ina e te mango.
Eje pa raua na kui ropa
Na pupute te manava i te tai e
Ka mate, E! E! E!

Eje Tata ma Toto uruu,
Manako ma te tamawine i te ropa ora;
Wakaveriveri i te povi mate,
Ma te tupapaku oki, E! E! E!

Tata and Toto fell into the sea
And were swallowed by the great shark.
They did not know
That by filling their stomachs with sea water
They would die, alas! alas! alas!

Tata and Toto will never again be lovers of maidens;
Young girls love only young men alive;
They hate dead men
And ghosts, alas! alas! alas!

XXIV
Tata and Toto

NOT long after the flying-fish expedition I sailed with King-of-the-Sky, William, Benny, and a dozen others in King-of-the-Sky's great sixty-foot canoe for Tema Reef. We started early in the morning with a fresh beam wind; by nine o'clock the island had sunk beneath the horizon and we were alone with empty sea stretching away to the horizon on all sides of us. The moment land had disappeared, the great canoe seemed no larger than a cockle-shell; the waves lapped dangerously near to the tops of the gunwales, all but toppling into the canoe; and that is the curious thing about Polynesian canoes: the water always laps just to the tops of the gunwales, no matter whether the canoe is shallow or deep, whether empty or heavily laden.

King-of-the-Sky's craft seethed through the water, throwing spray from its peculiar torpedo-shaped bow, riding the waves with a serpentine motion, for, being made of many parts lashed together, it has flexibility.

Two hours later King-of-the-Sky rose from his seat by the mast and moved to the bow to watch for Tema Reef, which is twenty miles from Puka-Puka. As we rose on the back of a great sea he shouted the opening lines of the Tema Reef chant, which is the same as crying, "Reef-ho!"

I soon caught my first glimpse of it: a pillar of spray rising geyserlike into the air and subsiding, leaving a cloud of mist hanging over the sea. It was a strange sight to behold in that deep and lonely ocean. As we drew nearer, the base of the pillar of spray spread out; other smaller spray pinnacles appeared, and gradually a long line of breakers was revealed on either side of the central geyser. That was the Tema Reef I had seen several years before from the deck of the *Tiaré*.

By midday we were alongside. The reef is a round plateau of coral more than half a mile in diameter and rising to within three feet of the surface. There

is no land there, not so much as a coral boulder showing above the sea, but the iron stem of some nameless vessel, red with rust, is embedded in the living coral. There has never been a recorded shipwreck on Tema Reef, for any ship lost there is lost with all hands. The breakers wash across the reef in a thousand whirlpools of raging foam, to meet in the center with an impact that can be heard from a great distance, rising in a pillar of spray fifty feet and more in height.

Countless sea birds circled overhead with clamoring cries heard faintly above the roar of the surf. The noise was so great that we had to shout at the top of our voices to be heard at the other end of the canoe. The birds, old William told me, are the souls of the ancient inhabitants of Tema who now retire to Nassau and Puka-Puka of a night, but fish by day over the remains of their once fertile island. One old frigate bird was perched on the iron ship's stem; perhaps he embodied the soul of Tema's last king. At any rate, he took his toll from the other birds, swooping down on the fishing terns and making them disgorge their catch to fill his capacious royal paunch.

Our nearness to the reef made me uneasy. King-of-the-Sky sailed calmly along it on the very edge of the combers till we reached the lee side of the shoal, where we lowered our sails. Benny took the coral-boulder anchor to the bow, while the others paddled straight for the reef so that he might drop it in shallow water where it would find good holding ground. On they paddled until we were in the steep seas which rise to break on the coral, and it seemed to me that in another instant we must be dashed to a certain death.

I held my breath, suppressing a cry. Just then Benny heaved the anchor onto the reef, and the canoe was paddled backward. A great sea rolling up behind us lifted our stern high in air until it seemed that we must all spill into the sea. I closed my eyes; my muscles were tense.

"Paddle! Paddle!" King-of-the-Sky yelled, and I could hear the paddles sing as they flashed through the water. Then the canoe righted itself and we were safe beyond the combers.

"If we had been a foot closer in we would all have been killed," Benny shouted with a laugh.

"It's nothing to laugh about," I replied sharply, but my words were lost in the thunder of the seas and the screeching of the sea-birds overhead.

We fished about fifty yards from the reef in as many fathoms of water. Any bait served. We weighted our lines with small pieces of coral brought for the purpose, using a slip-knot, so that when the baits were down to the required depth we had only to jerk the line to free them from the weights. No sooner were our hooks freed than great fish gulped the baits ravenously: rock grouper, barracuda, jacks, snappers, albacore. Our only trouble was with the sharks, for they circled about our canoe in schools of hundreds, often snapping the fish from our lines before they were half-way to the surface. Old William cursed them in four languages, and Benny sputtered "ifs" by the score. Luckily, King-of-the-Sky hooked a monster tiger shark, brought him to the surface, killed him, and sank him with a piece of coral tied to his tail. While his brethren were tearing him to pieces we managed to bring up half a dozen fine fish. We continued at our sport till sundown, when the canoe was well loaded.

When we were ready to return I moved casually into the bow and started pulling in on the anchor line, for I had been thinking of the danger of dragging in that coral boulder and of the horror of a panic-stricken death on Tema Reef. My knife was unclasped and thrust into my belt. When we were half the distance to the reef I unceremoniously cut the line, pretending not to hear the roars of profanity from old William. Then I turned brazenly, shrugged my shoulders, and said it was too late to growl; I would give King-of-the-Sky a fine piece of store rope in the place of his lost line. This quieted him somewhat, but every now and then, all the way home, he would break into a lament over his lost sennit, even, I believe, shedding a few tears over it.

King-of-the-Sky steered us home by the stars. The canoe was six inches deeper in the water, but still the water lapped just to the tops of the gunwales.

I thrust a paddle between my seat and the outrigger support and leaned back against it, closing my eyes. But I did not sleep, for presently King-of-the-Sky started one of the age-old chants of Puka-Puka—one of the songs that have already taken considerable space in these memoirs, but which deserve it,

I think, because of their importance in island life. On Puka-Puka it is impossible to catch a fish, kiss a maiden, climb a coconut tree, or play marbles without a chant to describe the action. And as I have already related, it is not only the ancient chants they sing, but others composed from day to day by people now living on the island.

But King-of-the-Sky's chant was of events so far in the past that they had long since become mythical. One by one the others joined in, and even the great canoe seemed to shake the spray from her bows in time with the rhythm as we skimmed over the moonlit undulations of the Pacific.

II

A thousand years ago—so the epic went—Tema Reef was a fertile island, the richest of all the atolls, and inhabited by a race of supermen who were the descendants of the seventy hero-gods. The earth-spirit who guarded it was a son of Orion (Tautoru), the mighty warrior whose yearly risings foretold the abundance of the harvest.

The people of Tema had foods unknown to the other atolls, for much guano was there, and the canoe-voyagers had brought breadfruit, mangos, plantains, taro, and other foods from far-off high islands.

The women of Tema were the fairest of all island women, fat, oily-skinned, and the best makers of tapa-cloth and pandanus mats in all the world.

The men of neighboring islands became jealous of the Temans, they coveted their fine taro-beds, their groves of breadfruit trees, and their beautiful fat women. So they came together, the warriors of Puka-Puka, of Nassau, of Manihiki, and of Rakahanga, and held a council of war where it was decided to surprise Tema, kill the men, and carry off the women for their wives.

They met at the appointed time on Nassau: one hundred double war canoes and three thousand warriors. At night they feasted; there was much drinking and merriment. The earth-spirit of Tema, who loved carousals, heard from afar the songs and laughter of the people on Nassau. He came swiftly to join the feast. But when soaring among the clouds above the island he caught a glimpse of the clubs and spears of the warriors, and heard the priests praying for victory, and thus knew this would be no peaceful gathering. The earth-spirit alighted in a coconut-palm, where he listened to the priests and warriors. There he heard of the proposed attack upon his island. At this he hurried away to consult the earth-spirits of the enemy islands. Each of them said: "I have had no part in this. Our children are mad. Take such action as seems best to you."

So the earth-spirit of Tema returned to his island in deep thought.

In three days there was to be held on the island of Tahiti the great feast of the rising of Orion, his father, and three days hence the attack on his island was to be made. He could not miss the feast in honor of his father, nor leave his island unprotected in his absence.

Then he remembered the vicious eel-god, Kalomaro, who lives in the bottom of the sea. He decided to call on him for help. He found the eel-god in the deepest sea, drowsing, his mouth gaping open so that huge fish might mistake it for a cave and enter, furnishing him a meal.

"Health to you!" cried the earth-spirit. "Are you living?"

"Alas! yes," grumbled the eel-god; "but I am in great trouble. I have grown so much in the past thousand years that my cave is too small for me. I cannot get out, for my tail is caught in the rocks. Alas! Alas!" and he went on lamenting the difficulties which rose from this unhappy circumstance.

"I will help you," said the earth-spirit, "but you must do me a favor in return." He then told him of the war to be made upon his island, and asked that the eel-god do this and this. The eel agreed, and the earth-spirit went a day's journey into the cave and found the place where the eel's tail was held fast by a submarine range of mountains. He broke them apart and freed the eel.

By the time he had returned to the eel's great head another day had come. "I cannot stay longer," said the earth-spirit. "To-morrow is the feast in honor of my father and I must go at once. Do not forget your promise."

"But how can I manage it?" grumbled the eel-god. "I have not seen the sun for centuries, and the light would blind me."

"Keep your head deep in the sea," replied the

earth-spirit. "Let your tail float on the surface and do as I have directed."

The great eel kept his promise. With his tail he lashed the sea to foam. After the first mighty sweep the waves rose higher than had ever been seen. At the second sweep they rose as high as the coconut-palms of Puka-Puka, and the hundred canoes and the three thousand warriors were all destroyed. The eel-god with his head buried two miles beneath the sea did not know how great a storm he had caused.

A third time his tail swept through the sea, and then the waves, touching the clouds and moving straight on Tema, crashed down, washing the island bare to its coral foundation, sweeping the guano, the taro-beds, the breadfruit groves, and the fine fat women all into the sea. Nothing remained—not a single palm-tree, not a single grain of sand. But two men who were fishing on the lee side of the island were miraculously saved. They clung to their canoes, although they were washed many miles from the island, and when the seas had subsided they bailed out their canoes and climbed in.

One of these men was Tata: it was he who paddled south to Nassau. The other was called Toto: it was he who paddled north to Puka-Puka.

The eel-god yawned, withdrew his great body into the depths of the sea, and went to sleep.

After the feast of Orion the earth-spirit returned to Tema, where he found only a barren reef washed by the sea. The souls of his people were wailing and calling with lonely voices blown about by the wind.

The earth-spirit wept for twenty years. Then he cried to the great earth-mother, who heard his lament:

"Behold, in the great loneliness of this place the spirits of my dead children are crying piteously. Transform them into sea-birds, O earth-mother, that they may soar over this reef in years to come, waiting for the waves to build again their island."

The earth-mother heard his petition and the souls of the Temans became white terns.

King-of-the-Sky's chant ended with the customary wail, dying slowly away. I opened my eyes with a start, aware that all was silent save for the slapping of little waves along the gunwales and the wind humming softly in the rigging. A somber-looking cloud had humped his back ominously above the horizon directly to windward, warning us that a squall was coming our way. I stared at it with some misgiving, for we were overloaded, and, as I have before mentioned, the waves were lapping along the tops of the gunwales. But remembering how the ancients had sailed for thousands of miles in such canoes, I felt easier. Turning to King-of-the-Sky, I asked: "What became of the two men who were saved? You said one paddled to Nassau and the other to Puka-Puka."

King-of-the-Sky gazed straight before him for a moment without speaking, as though he had not heard me. He shifted his huge body a little and grasped his steering-paddle more firmly; then, with a voice like the bellowing of a bull, a stentorian roar that must have been heard in the three villages, he chanted the gruesome legend of Tata and Toto.

III

It was Tata who made his way to Nassau, where, with a wife transformed from a *Ti* leaf by the earth-spirit of that place, he repopulated the island. Toto, upon arriving at Puka-Puka, stole him a wife from Leeward Village and settled on Frigate Bird Islet. There he became a great superman and no one dared to molest him. He had many children.

As Tata and Toto grew old they yearned to visit their native land; so, unbeknown to each other, they both set sail for Tema in small one-man canoes. There they met, and great was their sorrow at seeing that Tema was now only a barren reef. They had suspected this, and for this reason had not before returned to see with their own eyes the lonely shoal which had once been a beautiful island and their home.

When they has ceased weeping they set to fishing, for they were practical men who knew that lamentations would not fill their stomachs.

Toto caught one fat albacore after another, while Tata caught nothing but sharks. Toto, being a proud and vain person, cried: "Oh, Tata of Nassau! Do you, like the Rarotongans, eat shark meat? This is strange, for our ancestors ate no sharks, and we of Frigate Bird Islet dine only on the finest albacore. It must be the shark meat that makes you so thin."

Tata, being an envious person, said nothing, but a great hatred for Toto sprang up in his heart.

At that moment another great albacore swallowed Toto's hook, while at the same instant another shark, so old that he had barnacles on his back, viciously seized Tata's hook, broke the line and carried it with him to the bottom of the sea. Tata had no more hooks and lines, for the sharks had broken them one after another.

Toto roared with laughter as he pulled his fine fat albacore over the side of his canoe.

"Ah, Tata!" he cried, "what a pity! If you had caught that shark your wife and all your brats would have had plenty of food for a month. Here," he added lifting a very small, thin fish from his canoe, "take that one home to your wife, so that she will think you as great a fisherman as Toto!"

Tata paddled his canoe straight at Toto. "I will have your fish," he said, "and your life as well!"

He leaped into Toto's canoe and they fought so furiously that first Tata fell before Toto's blows and then Toto before Tata's. But in the great struggle the canoe was upset and the two men, clinched in one another's arms, sank into the sea. There a great white shark, who had arranged for this by scaring the albacore away from Tata's hook, gobbled them both down at a gulp.

That was the end of Tata and Toto in their earthly bodies; but to this day, if a belated fisherman has not left Tema Reef by moonrise, he will hear their ghosts taunting one another, and he will see the shadowy figure of the great white shark hovering far below, ready to eat their spirits as he has done every night for a thousand years . . .

Of a sudden the squall struck us. We lowered our mainsail and crept slowly on our course with a luffing

foresail. I ducked my head and listened to the wind screaming in the rigging. On a schooner it would have been nothing, but in our overloaded canoe it seemed that the furies had been let loose, or better, that the old eel-god had risen a second time from the depths of the sea to lash the surface with his twenty-mile tail.

But it passed, as all things do, and I was roused from my huddled position by the sound of Benny's voice: "This is the passage, King-of-the-Sky. Lower the foresail."

I looked up to find Puka-Puka Islet with its reef but a hundred yards away. A few lights flared in the village, and along the windward reef were a dozen torches where men were spearing lobsters.

It was about 2 A.M. when we pushed the canoe into the white sand before Central Village. Every one was awake, and more so than usual, for the news had spread that the Tema fishermen had returned. A hundred people were awaiting us on the beach, all too anxious to lend a hand, carrying the canoe to its blocks, and taking the fish to King-of-the-Sky's house.

Then came the division of the catch. There were fourteen of us in the canoe, the canoe itself counted for one share, one sail for another, and the other shares went to those who had loaned another sail, a mast, a piece of sennit, some hooks, fishlines, a bunch of drinking-nuts, and so on, totaling at least fifty shares.

Every now and then while King-of-the-Sky was dividing the catch he would throw a fish to one of the onlookers, saying in an offhand manner to the rest of us: "She's my old aunt; it would be wrong for me to be stingy with her," or, "She married my wife's sister's husband's nephew. I should be eternally shamed if I were to forget her." Or again, as he tossed away the largest of our albacore: "That's for my wife; she's always sticking her fingers in! But what can we do? Women always get the best of us."

"So they do," grumbled old William, seizing a great barracuda in one hand and a twenty-pound albacore in the other. "There's my old woman"—with this he tossed the fish to old Mama—"getting two of the best fish in the catch and we can't do a thing about it!"

"Alas!" sighed Benny as he chose two fat grouper and tossed them to his wife, "if it wasn't for the miserable woman who calls me husband, these two fish would not be lost to us."

By the time the division was completed we fishermen found that there were no fish for us, although our wives, children, and distant relatives were well supplied, from whose portions we might choose our own later.

While Desire and Little Sea were broiling our three-in-the-morning meal, I heard King-of-the-Sky bellowing out the story of how I had cut his fine sennit line. The next day I gave him a piece of manila rope worth much more than his sennit. It was some two weeks later, when he had returned from another Tema Reef excursion, that he woke me in the small hours of the morning to tell me that he had salvaged his lost sennit line. He had narrowly escaped being eaten by Tata and Toto's voracious white shark, being washed to perdition over the reef, and having his head bashed in on the sharp coral; nevertheless, he had gotten his line all right and was as proud of his exploit as he had every reason to be.

XXV

The Puka-Puka Wireless Station

Wi inangaro 'u ma te piani
Yao wakatangi i te wawine,
Waka ma wakiwaki rua tenga
Tangi pe te tangi o te upaupa.

Wi inangaro 'u ma te tamaka
Tangi pe te kiore koa mamae;
Ya wakalonga te wawine
I taku yaelenga ma te oire,
I taku yaelenga ra te vao.

Give me a noisy new mouth organ
To play before the village maidens,
While I beat my thighs together,
Playing the tune of the dance.

Give me a pair of new red shoes,
Noisy shoes that squeak like a rat;
All the maidens will hear me
As I stroll through the village,
As I stroll through the groves.

—*From* "Mako Oko-oko" (*Puka-Puka customer's chant*).

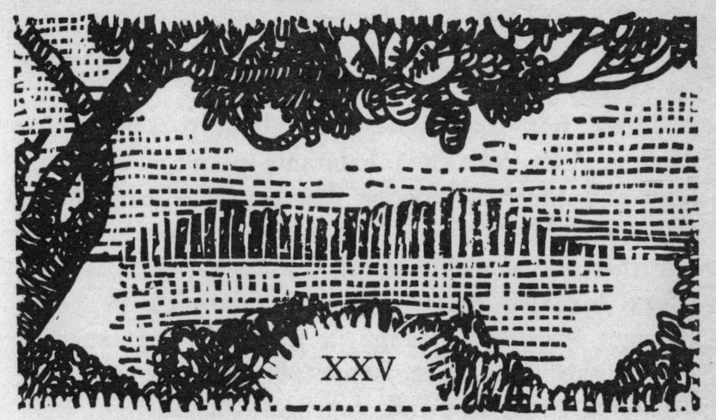

The Puka-Puka Wireless Station

MY neighbors having returned from one of their periodical copra-making expeditions to the neighboring islets, I found myself for several days with enough to do. About twenty tons of copra had been dried, most of which belonged collectively to the villages, for, as I have said, there is no private ownership of land on Puka-Puka. Each man is given his share of nuts to prepare and receives his portion of money or trade goods derived from the sale of the copra. But after the villages have made their collective lots, the remaining coconuts are divided. Some are used as food and the remainder split and the meat dried into individual batches of copra.

I had two village batches—from four to six tons each—to weigh, as well as several hundred individual bags, and paid for it at the rate of one penny (British) per pound. The nuts are remarkably uniform in weight, two of them being required to make a pound of copra, so that the natives receive an average of a half-penny per nut.

There was some wrangling about the price, for even on Puka-Puka the inhabitants wake up sufficiently now and then to wonder whether they cannot get more for their copra and pay less for trade goods. On this occasion Windward Village held back its copra for two months, losing about 10 per cent through further shrinkage in weight. They expected me to raise the price, some of the more sanguine dreaming about five and sixpence a pound.

I explained to them again and again that I could pay only a penny a pound, the current price all through the islands at the time of Viggo's last visit. "Yes," they replied, "but maybe the price has risen since Viggo was here." "And maybe it's gone down," I said. However, they would not listen and still refused to sell their copra.

I became rather annoyed at this foolishness, and after thinking matters over I decided to have some sport with the Windward Villagers. All the natives had heard of wireless telegraphy from the missionaries, or from some native who had been as far as Rarotonga, where he had gaped at the aërial while some "civilized" Rarotongan had related weird stories of the *tua-tua reva* (air talk). To a Puka-Pukan, of course, such a thing is sheer magic.

Knowing this, I had Benny stretch some wires from the roof of my store to that of the school-house. Then I rigged up a mass of meaningless wires, flashlight batteries, boxes and tins painted red, green, and yellow, bolts and gadgets of all sorts. Then I fastened a string from a clicker on the table to a pedal beneath it, so that I could make the clicker "speak" by working my foot up and down. My phonograph supplied motive power to turn various clockworks and whatnots.

When all was ready I let it be known that I had constructed a wireless so as to pass my evenings in conversation with my friends in Tahiti and the Cook Islands, and with my great personal friend William Cowboy, the famous movie star in the United States. I further explained that I would publish a daily bulletin of news from Rarotonga and other parts of the world.

My neighbors were so astonished and excited that no one slept that day. The store was crowded, and two or three natives who had been to Rarotonga took advantage of the opportunity to shine, explaining to the others what a wireless was, and minutely describing the mechanism. They declared that my wireless was exactly like the one in the great station at Rarotonga.

I started the thing going. It ticked merrily, and Benny, standing behind the gear, intermittently pressed a flashlight button behind some red tissue paper to give the appearance of high voltage current. As the wireless "talked" I wrote the messages on a slip of paper. One message caused me to pull a very long face. It was a message from London, which I wrote out in native, of course, and posted on the door. The translation is as follows:

"London, England, April 26, 19—. The price of copra has fallen to a half-penny per pound. The warehouses are full of copra and there are no purchasers. Warning has been sent to the traders of Cook Islands to buy no more copra this year."

The next day Windward Village came to me in a body to weigh in their copra. I declined, saying that, of course, I could not possibly buy it in view of the news received from London. The village fathers met that night and there was a long and violent discussion. Those who had been against the idea of holding out for higher prices now had their innings, and the opinions they expressed of the more grasping members of the settlement were as vigorous as they were picturesque and uncomplimentary. I kept all the fathers on pins and needles for a week, when a message came through to the effect that while the copra market was still unsteady, prices had again risen to a penny per pound. That same afternoon I purchased Windward Village's copra and the following day dismantled the wireless station, owing to the fact that the batteries had given out.

II

"I want a pair of shoes."

Abel (Abera), a village buck of Windward Settlement, was the prospective purchaser.

I produced some footgear that shone beautifully with a coat of shellac. "Here you are, Abel," I said. "These are the kind of shoes that all the young men of Rarotonga and Tahiti wear. And William Cowboy (William S. Hart) will have no other kind. They are the very finest shoes that can be bought anywhere."

For some time Abel stared vacantly at them; then he asked: "Do they squeak?"

"Squeak!" I exclaimed, forgetting myself for the moment; "of course they don't squeak!"

"Then I don't want them," he said, shaking his head decisively. "What is the good of shoes that don't squeak? I want noisy shoes so that people will hear them and admire them when I go to church."

I perceived my error at once, and brought out another pair, exactly like the first, for I carry only one line of shoes.

"I see, Abel, that you are a sensible customer, and you have a mind of your own: you know exactly what you want. I can't shuffle off any second-rate, silent shoes on you. Now, then, if you want a pair of the finest squeaking shoes, that can be heard a hundred yards off, here are the very ones!"

Abel made his purchase and left, and the next Sunday I saw him walking to church in the midst of the clown parade, dressed in his necktie, his derby hat, and his fine new shoes which squeaked as loudly as all the rats on Puka-Puka squeaking together. His face beamed when he noted the impression he was making on the young ladies, particularly on Everything's fair and rotund daughters, who were intimate friends of his. Such are the blessings of civilization brought to benighted savages by South Sea Island traders.

III

"I need a new mouth organ," said Bones, the superannuated "lady-killer," who has the honor of being the father of Letter and Table-Salt. His head is bald except for a wiry fringe around the base of his skull; his nose, like old William's, is very large, and rheum is perpetually oozing from his faded watery eyes. His clothes were in tatters and he was carrying a young pig, nursing it in his arms as though it were a baby.

"Here you are, Bones," I said; "a fine Japanese mouth organ, well-made, keyed true, and noisy: two and sixpence."

Depositing his pig on the counter he took the instrument, put it to his big sensual mouth, and breathed into it the most objectionable grunts and groans that could possibly be imagined. There was no tune to it, only amorous gruntings like those of some old satyr who had furnished music for Circe's revels. In fact, if there is, in these modern days, a living image of one of those evil earthly spirits who prowled through the forest glades in the world's youth, then, surely, it is old Bones of Puka-Puka.

XXVI
Bones—Champion

Kokoïi taku one ipuia
Ye piritia te tuakawa.
Kai lau au i te tautaua
Tu yemu-yemu mai na toa;
Pokia i te uru mai runga,
Kakaro ki muri ki to yinganga!
To ngutu kai te kere-kere!
  Pu te wui tane i te tori m'i runga,
  Ko Ivi te rakau tu!

Fence off a ring of coral sand
And call to me your wrestlers;
I will withstand the strongest of them!
One enters in: I spring, I thrust,
I clutch his body;
I fling him out
Beyond the ring of coral sand.
  He lies prostrate!
  I am Bones, the upright tree!

—*From* "Tira Kopoko no Ivi" (*Bones's wrestling chant.*)

Bones—Champion

ONE evening the villagers woke earlier than usual and gathered in the road before the store to wrestle. Although Puka-Pukans are the laziest people on earth, they are the champion wrestlers of the Cook and Line islands, a mediocre Puka-Pukan being able to throw any champion from another island.

The wrestling started with matches between boys from ten to fifteen years old, while little tots held bouts of their own. Soon half a dozen men from Windward Village stepped apart from the rest and drew themselves up in attitudes of defiance; it was a silent challenge to the men of the other villages. One by one, men from Central and Leeward Village met them and there was good sport for everybody, both spectators and contestants. A victory consisted in throwing an opponent or in lifting him from the ground; when one knee touches the ground the man has lost. No doubt this form of wrestling was adopted because of the nature of the ground, which is rough and gravelly and strewn with fragments of coral.

I was rather pleased to see George, the boastful one, thrown by an undersized Central Villager. George, of course, was ready with his excuse: he had been netting flying-fish the previous evening and had sprained both his wrists, he said. As soon as he had recovered from this accident he would take pleasure in throwing this Central Villager and all his friends and relatives.

King-of-the-Sky was present watching the sport, but he did not join it, for he was dressed in his brass-buttoned coat and trousers of billiard-table green, which had already served several generations of Sky-Kings. The cloth was wearing exceedingly thin in spots, and King-of-the-Sky was fully aware of this. I had often noticed that when dressed in his Sunday clothes he walked with the greatest circumspection. When about to sit down in church he would ease up the cloth about his knees and loosen it around the seat of his trousers in order to avoid any embarrassing accident.

It is the custom at the wrestling-matches for the people to come dressed in their Sunday best. Scratch-Woman was there in her ancient lace dress, striped socks, and high-heeled shoes—not that she planned to wrestle, but she never lost an opportunity to display her mildewed finery. Ears wore his golfer's knicker-bockers and wrestled in them with Ura, his chief, who was rigged out in his commodore's coat, epaulets and brass braid. Glory where glory belongs—the commodore's coat soon lay prostrate in the dust. There was an amusing sequel to this episode the following day. Ura called a special meeting of his council, where he officially fired Ears from the force. This sort of thing had happened before, and Ears, as usual, refused to be dismissed. But this mattered little; Ura had performed the act of dismissal and thus regained his self-esteem.

Presently who should come to the contest but old Bones, his new mouth organ conspicuously displayed stuck in a flower wreath around the crown of his hat.

"There's the champion," said Desire. "He can throw any two men on the island."

I laughed, thinking that this was her idea of a joke.

"It's true," she said, seriously; "Bones is the best wrestler on Puka-Puka."

Still I didn't believe her, and was astonished to see the old satyr walk to the center of the ring and stand there defiantly, his arms akimbo and his legs spread apart. I laughed aloud and Bones glanced at me with an injured expression in his watery eyes. I noticed that his Pantagruelian nose was swollen to twice its ordinary size, due to a monstrous boil, fiery-red except the center, which was white. My fingers itched to lance the thing; it was just ripe for opening.

At first no one accepted Bones's challenge; but presently a stalwart Windward Villager, about six feet four and all muscle, stepped forward.

"Poor old Bones!" I said, but Little Sea replied, "Just wait. Bones will throw him. Look at his arms."

Heretofore my attention had always been fixed on Bones's face, for it was horribly fascinating in its ugliness. But now I examined his body and was amazed to find that his hands actually reached to his knees. And the rolls of hard muscle on his arms reminded me of a mule's hind leg. The shoulders, although sadly stooped, were powerful and easily twice as broad as mine.

Bones smiled fatuously when the Windward man stepped before him. The latter made a grab for the champion's leg, but at the same instant a long gorilla-like arm shot out and caught him by his sennit belt. The Windward Villager, failing to grasp Bones's leg, raised his arm quickly in an attempt to get hold of the nape of his neck. In doing so his hand accidentally struck the champion's nose. The blow did all that my lancet could have done. The boil exploded, much to the defilement of the old man's face.

Bones yelled with pain, and the next instant we saw the Windward Villager rise from the ground, sail through the air, and land with a tremendous thud half a dozen yards away.

"There, damn it!" cried the feeble old man; "if you hadn't smashed my boil, I'd have let you down easy!"

His face, as I have said, was ugly enough at best, and in view of what had just happened to his nose—but enough of that.

"Good work, Bones!" I said as he went past me, homeward.

He smiled hideously, shaking his head.

"Ah me!" he said, "I am growing old, I fear. Six months ago I could have tossed him on to the village church."

XXVII

Try-It's Classes

Toku tama yaelenga ki te apii,
P'u to nga manako pakari.
Ka koni oki, oto, pata-pati,
Aué! te marama na toku tama!

My child goes to school,
My child has learnt all wisdom.
He can sing, dance, and play marbles also;
Oh! the wisdom of my child!

—*From* "Mako Apii" (*school chant*)

XXVII

Try-It's Classes

ACCORDING to the salutary regulation laid down by the Rev. Johns during a former visit to Puka-Puka, no child shall sleep between the hours of 8 and 10 A.M., for at this time Sea Foam, assisted by Try-It (Tamata), teaches the children to read the Bible and vainly attempts to initiate them into some of the mysteries of arithmetic.

School opens with one hundred and twenty-odd children lined up before the school-house. Sea Foam, followed by Try-It, a tall, gloomy-faced individual reminding one of the immortal *Ichabod*, marches down the line, examining the hair, eyes, and noses of the children, and when, as often happens, there are evidences of failure to wash faces, the culprits are sent down to the lagoon to attend to the matter. When they reach the lagoon the children quite naturally wade in, not having any clothes to get wet. They have such a good time splashing about that they forget all about school. Anyway, school is a foolish business, and it's much more fun swimming. The result is that Sea Foam sees no more of them that day. He doesn't mind; he is glad to be rid of the brats, for, as he often says, there are plenty of scholars, anyway.

Following inspection comes a few minutes of callisthenics, an innovation of the Rev. Johns. Imagine teaching these superbly healthy savages callisthenics! The parents stare perplexedly from their houses while their children go through the motions with grunts and sighs. *"Vuni—tooi—treei!"* cries Sea Foam, giving them the time. A quarter of an hour later they file into the school-house to read the Bible.

Sometimes Sea Foam takes a nap in the school-house—in fact, he often does—whereupon all the children go home; and when the good parson wakes he finds that it is evening and he has long been alone. He puts his books under his arm and strolls home, stopping at the store for a moment to have a chat with me. School-teaching is a great burden, he informs me; often his whole day is taken up over his books, leaving him little time to search for suitable texts and quotations for his Sunday sermon.

There is a small thatched hut near the more pretentious coral-lime school-house; it has open sides and a few coconut logs for benches. There Try-It herds his class of youngsters for two long hours each morning. Sometimes he instructs them in the mysteries of the a-b-c's; at others he hammers the science of numbers into their heads by sing-song repetitions of "One-times one is one; one times two is two." This is taught

in English, so that the children may not have the remotest idea of what they are learning. At other times he reads a chapter from the Bible; and at still other times he, too, takes a nap.

One morning I looked on secretly at one of Try-It's sessions. He sat with his back to one of the roof-posts, listening, perhaps, to the singsong of the children, and again perhaps not. A faint breeze fanned the cheeks of his charges and caressed his own stubby jowls. A soporific silence reigned in the main school-house where Sea Foam was supposed to be at work.

Try-It turned his back on the children and for a time stared vacantly across the lagoon. Perhaps he was thinking. The sing-song of the scholars gradually died away until silence also reigned in the thatched hut. Several youngsters stole quietly out to play marbles; others leaned back against their coconut logs and instantly fell asleep.

Try-It dug his hand into his overalls pocket and brought forth a mouth organ. Putting it to his lips, he breathed out sleepy strains that made the very chickens scratching about the doorway drowsy. A little tot in the back row stood up to do a little dance, then sank to the gravel floor and fell asleep. Several others slipped out to join the marble-players. Try-It played on. I could see his long legs beneath his table, doing a sort of dance by themselves in time to the music.

Of a sudden he jerked up his head as though he had just remembered that he was a schoolmaster and that school was then in session. All of his scholars had gone except those who had fallen asleep on the floor. Try-It did not appear to be greatly surprised. He tiptoed softly out so as not to wake the sleeping youngsters, and strolled home, the mouth organ still at his lips. By that time I too had become so drowsy that it was all I could do to stumble across the road into the store. Benny was snoring on the counter; Little Sea and Desire had fallen asleep over a game of checkers. I glanced outside once more; the village street was blazing in the sunlight and not a soul to be seen in the length of it. I lay down on a mat, intending to read for a few moments, but the book fell from my hands before I had reached the end of the first paragraph. It's a hard life, that of a trader on Puka-Puka.

II

One evening, after a hard day's work at the schoolhouse, Sea Foam dropped in at the store. I could see that he had some request to make, for his bearing was both dignified and obsequious. It was this way, he explained: The Rev. Johns was expected to visit the island shortly, and he, Sea Foam, wished to make a fine showing in the school. He remembered that on Rarotonga the school-children sang certain patriotic songs in English which greatly pleased the missionaries. If I, Ropati, would consent to teach the children of Puka-Puka some such song, he, Sea Foam, would esteem it a very great favor indeed.

I readily agreed, and the next morning, donning a clean singlet and a pair of trousers, I entered the school-house just as the session was beginning.

I wrote the verses of "God Save the King" on the blackboard and then had the children repeat the lines of the first stanza after me. They quickly memorized it, although they were quite ignorant of its high-minded import. In three days' time they had memorized the three stanzas.

Then I began to teach them the air. I played it over at least a score of times on my accordion to impress it well upon their minds. Then I rose, swung my hands bandmaster fashion, and said: "One, two, three, sing!"

Good Lord! or Carramba! as old William would say. I might as well have tried to teach them "Parsifal." For a month I persevered and for a month I completely failed. Even Sea Foam gave up hope. The children simply could not grasp the melody, but must chant the words in their own guttural manner, with grunts and weird arpeggios. The bars accompanying the words, "Send him victorious, happy and glorious," they sang after a fashion, though roaring them out with barbarous gusto, like a war-cry. But the rest was impossible, and in the last line the chorus dwindled away in awful discords.

I then tried various other songs, "The Wearing of the Green," "Hail Columbia," "Marching Through Georgia," but the result was the same.

After two months of intermittent effort I decided to give up the business altogether, for Viggo was expected any day, and he would bring the Rev. Johns. But one evening when I was sitting with Benny, old William, Little Sea, and Desire, I chanced to pick up my accordion and finger the keys idly, singing to myself. My friends listened patiently, as they always do, although I can see that they are bored, European or American music being altogether too strange for them to understand. I went from one song to another as they happened to come to me, and presently found myself singing the rollicking old slaver's chantey, "It's Time for Us to Go":

A quick run to the south we had, and when we made the bight,
We kept the offing all day long and crossed the bar at night.
Six hundred niggers in the hold and seventy we did stow,
And when we'd clapped the hatches on 'twas time for us to go.

> Time for us to go,
> Time for us to go,
> And when we'd clapped the hatches on
> 'Twas time for us to go.

Old William pricked up his ears, and Benny leaned forward to repeat something vaguely like "Time for us to go." To my astonishment Desire hummed the air with scarcely a mistake.

Instantly the thought came to me that this was the song to teach the school-children. If Desire could hum it, they could learn it, and I realized that it was the kind of air they would have least difficulty with. The next morning I returned to the school-house and before midday had the whole mob roaring:

> Time for us to go,
> Time for us to go,
> When the money's out and the liquor's done,
> Why, it's time for us to go.

I have since had certain prickings of conscience because of this affair, for when the Rev. Johns came, and Sea Foam had the school-children rise and bellow out this slaver's chantey, the missionary was very much upset. I have a warm place in my heart for the reverend, even though he is a little intolerant on the subject of clothing for the natives and such matters. He knew, of course, that I had taught the children this sinful song, but he never reproached me about it, or made the slightest reference to it in my presence. He merely told Sea Foam, later, that he was pleased to find the children learning English so rapidly, but on the whole he believed it would be better for them to learn no more secular songs. He preferred their singing hymns, "Nearer, My God, to Thee," and "Bringing In the Sheaves," in the native tongue.

XXVIII

Over the Reef

Na wakatere toku tima lel'i
Na p'u te wui wenua mamao.
E kapiki te meeti:
"E rangatira e! T'ia Puka-Puka!"
Tangi taua toku ove,
Wakatangi 'u i te pu,
Wakamaniania!
Ke tiri 'i taku vie
Ke wamumura ko te awi,
Wakakü te rangi koa pupuni i te 'u'i!

My beautiful vessel sails
To every distant land.
One day the mate calls:
"Captain! See! This is Puka-Puka!
Ring the bell!
Blow the horn!
Make a great noise!
Throw fuel on the fire
Making a great blaze
And filling all the sky with smoke!"

—*From* "Waiva Tangata" (*A Puka-Puka castle builder's chant*).

XXVIII

Over the Reef

A FEW months ago, while surf-boarding across the shallows near Windward Village, I was swept into a depression in the reef where a rapid current washed me through the breakers into the open sea. It was as much as my life was worth and I knew it.

The sun was just setting behind a heavy screen of storm clouds; half a gale chopped the sea to white-caps; and between me and the shore was a line of gigantic breakers raising their backs twenty feet above the jagged coral to crash with terrific violence the whole length of the reef. Even a Puka-Pukan would have considered it impossible to regain the shore.

I had clung to my surf-board, a piece of one by four planking, four feet long. It buoyed me up somewhat; otherwise I could not have survived three minutes in that frothy sea.

The news was yelled across the island and soon the beach was black with people; some of the stronger men were on the reef vainly trying to throw me pieces of wood. They watched me with morbid excitement, for they expected momentarily to witness my last agonies.

Three desperate chances were open to me. One was to swim round to the lee side of the island, a distance of about five miles. This was impossible; night was setting in and the gale increasing. Furthermore, my strength was rapidly ebbing in the fight for breath against the waves that constantly bashed against my face. Or I might wait for a canoe to cross the lagoon to the lee reef and come round to me. Only the largest of the canoes could have weathered that sea, and at least two hours would be needed to make the passage. I should be dead long before they could reach me.

The third chance was to swim straight for the reef, and this I did, without hope of getting across but with a strangely exhilarating determination not to give up my life without a struggle. I have sometimes had moments of absurd panic while swimming in deep water far out from shore, as when turtle-fishing with Benny; but now I was nerved by a sort of reckless courage and looked forward without fear to the coming fight, as though the combers were human enemies whom I should somehow injure before they crushed and buried me. When one believes that death is inevitable one is indifferent to everything except a final splendid demonstration of one's ego—at least, so it was with me that murky evening, a chip flung, buried, raised, derided by the relentless sea.

Coming within the grasp of the combers, I looked back again to see an immense wave about to hurl itself upon me. All my courage ebbed in an instant. The struggle was too hopeless; the contrast between that mighty wall of water and my puny self was too clearly apparent.

Then, strangely, my courage returned. I refused to lose this last opportunity for self-assertion. As the comber curled to fall, I dove straight into it as the only means of protecting myself from its impact.

I could feel the concussion as it hurled itself on the reef; the water became milky with foam, and I knew that I was being tossed about perilously close to the jagged coral.

Fighting my way to the surface, my head was buried in two feet of foam. I beat the water frantically, trying to raise myself above that layer of soft choking froth. My lungs were bursting when it had subsided sufficiently for me to gasp the fresh air.

I scarcely had time to empty and refill my lungs before another comber reared above me with the malice of a cat playing with a mouse.

Subconsciously I was fighting the greatest battle of all, suppressing an almost overpowering fear which prompted me to dive, fill my lungs with water, and put an end to the struggle. But consciously I was still exhilarated: I was ending my life with gusto, with almost sensual gratification.

The comber fell just as I was diving. Half-stunned, I was whirled around like a chip. I had a vague impression that my head had grazed the coral; in fact, as I afterward learned, a deep gash had been laid open half-way across my scalp. It now seemed that the end was at hand, for again there was the deep layer of light foam above my head. I held my breath, expecting to hear the peculiar hissing sound of the next toppling sea.

As the foam subsided, coughing and gasping for breath I exerted my last strength, making a few feeble strokes toward the reef, now but a few yards distant. Dimly I could see naked figures along the reef gesticulating frantically. I knew that they were warning me of the approach of the next breaker, but I didn't turn my head. There was nothing more that I could do. In my own mind I was already dead, for I had been through the terror of dying, and the final annihilating stroke had only been delayed for a few seconds, that was all. On the beach I saw a hazy line that seemed to waver and melt into blackness as I watched it. I knew it was the villagers standing as close as they could to get to me, watching the end.

There was now less than a fathom of water beneath me, and even though I had had the strength, I could not have dived. I heard the roaring of the oncoming comber; lights flashed in the darkness, and in that second I saw, with uncanny vividness, the form of my mother sitting in her arm-chair, quietly knitting and gazing up at me with her thoughtful, compassionate eyes.

I lived, of course, but it was a near thing. The last comber had buried me, hurled me across the reef, and rolled me like a log to a spot where the natives rushed out to grasp me.

I remember little of what followed, although I have a faint recollection of people carrying me inland, and of the great little Ura waving his arms and crying: "He is a superman (*toa*)! A Puka-Pukan would have been killed by the first wave!" My pride is so strong that I remember his words more vividly than any other circumstance. He was right: a Puka-Pukan would have philosophically allowed the first wave to kill him, not being sufficiently egotistical to make a final grandiose gesture in the face of death.

That night old William and Mama, Little Sea and Desire sat by my mat. Little Sea had my feet in her lap, massaging them. Desire sat huddled in a corner, whimpering. Mama stroked my forehead, while the whole night through William repeated the story of the incident, adding details with each narration, so that, long before dawn, he had placed me in the same class with Great Stomach, who flew over the sea. It was annoying, to say the least, to have the one thing I wished to forget dinned everlastingly into my ears.

I was aware of a cutting pain in my side and that my breath was coming laboriously, but this was nothing to the mental pain; for when I shut my eyes great combers would rise above me to hang there on the verge of breaking for moments at a time; then they would subside, giving place to others. They seemed to have human faculties and to be leering at me in a cruel, implacable manner. They were screaming that they had pounded the reefs of Puka-Puka for thousands of years and that no mere human should interrupt their endless toil even for a moment.

Toward morning I sent for my medicine chest and took five grains of opium. In a few minutes I was asleep.

I awoke in the evening, coughing up quantities of blood. The pain in my side had grown to a steady burning pang, aggravated by the least movement, and, when I coughed, forcing me to use all my strength to keep from screaming. I could still see the combers rising with horrible deliberation over my head, and I realized vaguely that all during my sleep I had been harassed by a dream-fugue of curling, crashing breakers.

About midnight, after a fit of coughing, I sank back on my mat to feel the pain gradually lessening. Dimness veiled my eyes, and it was with a feeling of immense relief that I awaited the approach of death. To this day I am more than half-convinced that I did die. At any rate, the watchers thought me dead, and all but one of them resigned me to the shades of the ancients.

Half an hour later I awoke, or was revivified. I was dimly conscious, and yet my whole body was as lifeless as though the blood had congealed in my veins. Only my mind functioned, refusing to give up life even though the body was stiff and cold. As though coming from an infinite distance, I could hear the death songs being chanted over me, the patter of footsteps as people ran back and forth on the road below, and the barely audible cry: "Ropati is dead! Ropati is dead!"

I believed that I was dead, and I remember the dim thought came to me that, after all, there is a life after death, a belief I had always scoffed at.

Little Sea and Desire were wailing, with their bodies thrown across my legs, and who but evil—or, rather, good old Bones, the village libertine, the most degenerate soul on the island, was leaning over me, absolutely refusing to give me up as he vigorously massaged my body with those powerful, gorilla-like hands of his. Without lecherous old Bones I am convinced that I would have died that night; but by some mysterious Polynesian method of massage (*tarome*), a method which I have often seen used to as much as bring a man out of the grave, Bones saved me. God—if there is one—bless his sinful old soul—if he has any.

Still the death chant went on much as it had over the body of Wail-of-Woe, and at last another half-hour passed before I was sufficiently restored to show signs of life. Consciousness had returned by imperceptible degrees. At first I was only dimly aware of something touching my body lightly. Then I associated this with Bones, whom I could vaguely see leaning over me. A tingling sensation suffused my muscles, much like that one feels when one's foot is asleep. It was at about this time that I blinked my eyes, bringing the death wail to an abrupt end and sending Bosun-Woman home, doubtless greatly disappointed at being balked in her expectation of revels over a

fine white corpse. I can still see the ghastly smile on her witchlike face as she turned to leave; and now, when I meet her in the village, she looks at me as much as to say: "Wait, Ropati—just wait! You fooled me once, but I'm in no hurry. I'll be laying you out one of these fine days."

What a lovable, incompetent nurse garrulous old Mama was! Little Sea and Desire could have taken much better care of me, but Mama would not hear of it. What! Allow two mere "drinking-nuts" and one of them no more than an undeveloped *koua*, to nurse me? Never! So dear old Mama settled herself comfortably in my house to attend to my wants.

In the height of my fever she fed me roast pork, lobster, taro pudding, and tinned beans; and when convalescent, arrowroot starch, eggs, and milk; but thanks to a reasonably good constitution and Bones's daily massaging, I managed to pull through, and in a month's time I could sit up and take notice of the world of Puka-Puka.

Once Jeffrey, the village witch-doctor, came to visit me with his bottles of noxious medicines and a leering, conceited smile on his lips. Possibly Bosun-Woman had sent him, aware of his skill at hastening the departure of the ailing. I sent him away with an outburst of curses that only old William could appreciate. The old heathen had increased respect for me from that time on, and I think I have never, either before or since, shown such profane versatility.

II

One day Mama was sitting by me embroidering with clumsy calloused hands a pillow-slip after her own design. Little Sea had taught her the trick, but Mama would have none of those foolish flower designs. She intended to present me with a pillow-slip which she herself had "composed." There were a dozen big fish chasing, and about to gulp, as many little fish. And there was a red coconut-palm growing, apparently, in the middle of a yellow sea. Two figures stood below it and two nuts were falling from the tree straight for the men's heads. Dear old Mama would laugh and slap her withered shank as she explained the import of the design.

I took up a book but failed to interest myself in it. Presently I asked Little Sea to bring me my photograph-album, and showed Mama various scenes and portraits.

One of the first pictures was of myself standing in a small boat holding an albacore in each hand.

"Oh!" cried Mama, clapping her hands, "a steamboat!"

"No, no, Mama," I said; "it's only a little fishing boat I once owned at Tahiti."

"But it's got a smoke-stack," said Mama.

"No, that's me, Ropati, standing in the boat."

Mama held the album at about two inches from her myopic eyes, studying the picture long and intently, muttering to herself the while. At last she shook her head in a skeptical manner. "Well, Ropati, it may be you, but it looks like a steamboat to me."

I turned the page to a photograph of my old Aunt Deborah, surrounded by her family of fifteen.

"Oh, a mountain!" cried Mama, after she had examined it for some time.

This may seem absurd, but it is precisely what old Mama said. She had very poor eyesight; furthermore, she had never in her life seen a photograph of any sort until I came to Puka-Puka, and although she knew nothing of either mountains or steamboats, except by hearsay, she was always likening the pictures in my books to one or the other.

"No, Mama," I explained. "That is my Aunt Deborah and her fifteen children. You see, the photographer arranged them so that the little ones are at the ends and the tall ones in the middle, so the outline is something like that of a mountain."

"Have you ever been on a mountain, Ropati?"

"Oh, yes, many times."

"Is a mountain as high as a coconut-tree?"

I turned through the pages, much to Mama's delight. She saw only mountains and steamboats, but took my word for it that most of the photographs were of my friends and relatives in America. There was Yancey, who kept a grocery store and who used to give me chewing-gum; and Doc Harry, who often came to our house for Sunday dinners, and Uncle Harvey and the Rev. Hezekiah—many more. It saddened me to think how far I had drifted from my old life and of the many years that had passed since I had last seen any of the dear ones at home.

I started describing to Mama the wonders of

America: its vast plains, its mountains, the mighty lakes and rivers, and the great highways stretching from coast to coast. "Just think, Mama," I said, "if you were to start walking from the Pacific Ocean across America, and could keep going day and night, it would take months to reach the Atlantic Ocean!"

"You mean, if you were to paddle across," said Mama.

"No," I said, "walk."

"But that's foolish! You couldn't walk across the lagoon."

"I've said nothing about a lagoon."

"But how could you cross an island without crossing the lagoon, unless you followed the reef, and that's not walking across it but around it."

Mama, never having seen any land but a coral atoll, could not conceive of an island without a lagoon; and of course, to her, America was nothing more than an atoll somewhat larger than Puka-Puka. For a long time I tried to explain, saying that there were mountains and plains where the lagoon should be; but she would always break in with the question: "But where *is* the lagoon, then?"

At last, somewhat exasperated, I said: "Damn it! There is no lagoon!"

"Goddam it! There ain't none!" roared old William, who was on the veranda. He had not heard the argument, but had caught my ejaculation. Being accustomed to swearing, particularly at Mama, in season and out of season, he could not let such an opportunity pass.

But Mama still persisted that there must be a lagoon somewhere. So I asked Little Sea to bring me a pencil and paper and drew for Mama the sketch of America Island, arranging matters as best I could so that she could see how things were. She studied the plan for at least ten minutes, while I painstakingly pointed out the different lands, explaining everything in minute detail. Presently she turned the chart upside down. She recognized the peninsula of Florida and the Isthmus of Panama as two smoke-stacks and decided that what I had drawn was really a lovely steamboat.

XXIX

The Ancient Dead

Kai yoki-yoki io,
Yu-yu mata ra.
Tipa! Tipa!
Ngarué! Ngarué!
Taiare ui!

Carry him above our heads,
Close to the sun's eye.
Shake him! Shake him!
Sway him! Sway him!
Fling him into his grave!

—*From* "Tira no te Ariki Mate" (*Burial shout for the dead king*).

The Ancient Dead

WILLIAM and I turned from the road and followed the private trail of Mr. Chair's society to where lies the largest of Puka-Puka's graveyards, near Central Village council house. William was carrying a solitary bottle of rum Viggo had brought from Tahiti, and we were looking for a secluded spot in which to enjoy it.

Coming to a lean-to beside one of the graves, William turned and said: "Goddam! Fine place! Bones and Benny will never find us here."

We crawled under the coconut thatch. Within was a space about six feet square covered with woven frond mats where the relatives of some dead man came, occasionally, to sleep. The high side of the lean-to was open and faced the clearing.

After a couple of pulls at the bottle, William started the conversation, saying, apropos of nothing: "Now that gravestone over there."

"What about it?"

"What about it! Puncture me! He was an ancestor of mine!"

"He was? What was his name?"

"Carramba! How should I know?"

"I should think, on an island like Puka-Puka, you would know your ancestors' names."

"Hell, no! This lubber died several hundred years ago; but I know he was one of my ancestors because the stone at the head of the grave leans a little to the left, while the one at the foot leans the other way. And I know by the stones along the sides that he was blind in one eye and had a fine set of teeth."

After this display of anthropological lore he was silent for a moment while he had another drink. Presently he said: "But that one next to him was a no-account man. He was white-headed when he died, which proves that he ate other people's coconuts. He married twice; had four children by his first wife and two by the second, and he had elephantiasis in both legs."

"What was his name?"

"He died hundreds of years ago, but I know he was a descendant of Tauperoa, Big Stomach's enemy. Of course any child knows that. It is shown by the kind of coral the stones are made from."

"How did you know the other particulars about him?"

William gave me a contemptuous glance.

"Hell and damnation! You got no eyes? What they teach you in the white man's school? Can't you see that the bottom of the headstone has been smoothed off? That shows as plain as day that he was white-headed. The two notches on the foot-stone mean that he had two wives, and the coral slabs along the sides, four on one side and two on the other, show the number of his brats. And anybody knows by the way the grave lies that he had big legs."

"And that ancestor of yours—how do you know he had only one eye?"

"Look at those sharp-pointed slabs along the sides: they show that he had a fine set of teeth."

"There's one stone missing—does that mean he had one tooth out?"

"You are one big fool!" said William scornfully. If he'd had a tooth out, do you suppose they would have put those stones there to show he had a fine set of teeth? That missing stone means he was blind in one eye."

"But couldn't those stones mean his children, like the ones on the other grave?"

The old man fairly singed me with curses for daring to have such a suggestion to offer. He gave me to understand that I was not qualified to have opinions in such matters. He broke off abruptly, shot out a long bony arm to grasp the rum bottle, which he concealed in the rags of his denim trousers. *"Shh!"* he whispered out of the corner of his mouth.

Old King Pirato was coming toward us through the groves. As soon as he was within hearing, William chanted:

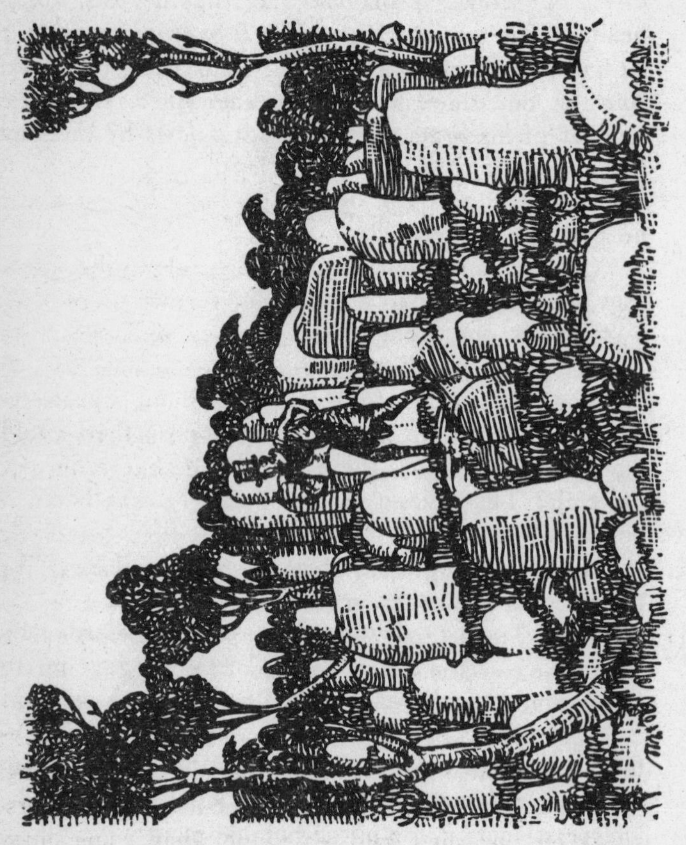

Kai yoki-yoki io,
Yu-yu mata ra.
Tipa! Tipa!
Ngarué! Ngarué!
Taiare ui!

Carry him above our heads,
Close to the sun's eye.
Shake him! Shake him!
Sway him! Sway him!
Fling him into his grave!

Little King Pirato, with the rags of a shirt hanging about his emaciated shoulders, turned sleepy eyes toward us, grinned foolishly, did a bone-stiff little dance and croaked: "Not for a few moons yet, O William." Then he went on his way, limping on one bare foot while the other, incased in a heelless, toeless, all but soleless shoe, was slapped bravely on the road.

And here am I speaking of King Pirato almost for the first time, when, by all the rules of courtesy, he should have appeared in the early chapters of these memoirs. Poor, inoffensive, incompetent, indolent Pirato! I have scarcely thought of him before. He is by birth the monarch of Puka-Puka, the possessor of a man-of-war officer's uniform, and has letters patent from Queen Victoria, vesting him with royal rights. How the little king loves to produce these letters with their tarnished gold seals, and what a fine show he makes in his superb uniform! I have no doubt that he could inflict capital punishment on the Puka-Pukans if an occasion should warrant it and he were so inclined. But he is too listless to rule even in little things, and so the authority has gone by default to Ura.

Pirato passed on, as he has since passed to an even dreamier world.

After another drink, old William proceeded to explain to me how kings are buried on Puka-Puka, for he had seen King Pirato's father interred fifty years before.

When the death chant has been wailed for two days and two nights, the king's body is carried through the villages, held above the people's heads by the nearest of his kin. When they arrive at the grave, which is very deep, they shout:

> Carry him above our heads,
> Close to the sun's eye.
> Shake him! Shake him!
> Sway him! Sway him!
> Fling him into his grave!

and at this point, with all their strength they hurl the body of their sovereign into the grave. If the royal corpse grunts when striking the bottom, the people are satisfied, for they believe that the spirits of his ancestors have heard him grunt with satisfaction, and they will be pleased that he has been properly buried. If, however, he fails to grunt, the body is lifted from the grave and the whole business is repeated, many times if necessary.

After this the king's eldest daughter descends into the grave and ties a cord of sennit about the body. She brings one end of it to the surface and the grave is then filled. When the earth has been mounded up, the king's daughter kneels on the mound, jerks the cord, and lays her ear to the ground, listening. After several jerks she may say that she has heard her father grunt, which is a sign that he is contented. But if she says that her father has made no sound, the body is disinterred and the entire ceremony repeated. As soon as the daughter is satisfied that her father has grunted, the ceremony is at an end, and all the men go fishing, knowing that they will make a fine haul, for all the spirits of the dead kings are pleased with them and will bring them luck.

William then returned to the pleasant topic of gravestones, explaining how each stone tells the story of the man buried beneath, even though it has no chiseled inscription. Thus a pointed headstone, three small ones on either side, and another painted one at the foot proclaim that a great fisherman is buried beneath. A square headstone with two little digits protruding from the corners means, for some strange reason, that the occupant of that grave was baldheaded. Other stones were unmistakably phallic symbols—Bones, very likely, will have such a stone if ever he dies, which is extremely improbable. An interesting volume could be written about the gravestones of Puka-Puka, for there are many kinds, and each village has its own symbolism.

"Carramba!" cried William, "I have decided on a fine stone for you, Ropati. It will tell about your cowboy adventures, your two Puka-Puka wives, and everything else!"

"William," I replied, evasively, "just look at that sunset! A salmon red like the tinned salmon I sell at the store for one and sixpence. By the way, do you like tinned salmon?"

"Blast me, no! Salmon is for women, beef for men. I will have another drink. But about your death chant: I have a part of it ready. It goes like this:

E kovi tikai aia i te uru u,
E kovi kai i te au kai katoa.
Lau t'i puroto, lau t'i povi,
P'u roa i te manava et'i.

A strong man for hunting was he,
A man who killed all the game.
Fifteen young ones, fifteen old ones,
Was the game of a night for him.

"Enough, William! More than enough!" I cried.

"Carramba! Yes, thirty should be enough for any man!"

"Thirty what?"

"Hell and damnation! What a question!" roared the old heathen.

II

Night set in, cloudless but dark. I stared out of the hut across the cemetery where the gravestones glimmered faintly under the light of the stars. Despite the rum I had drunk, a shiver ran down my spine. I imagined that I could see shadowy figures moving here and there among the stones.

I heard a gurgling sound from the darkness close

at hand. The old man smacked his lips as he set down the bottle.

"When you are an old lubber like me," he said, "you'll know all these old Puka-Pukans. Yes, and you'll see them too. Many's the night I have."

But little more was needed to excite my imagination to the seeing point. Already shadows seemed to be taking form around me, heads with empty eye-sockets and rows of gleaming white teeth; and flesh-covered forms as well—men with elephantiasis legs and hair so white that it gleamed with phosphorescent light.

"Now there was Mauta a Tau," mumbled the old man, as I watched more of the ancient Puka-Pukans rising from their graves. "He was a great fisherman, and he married King Rauta's daughter, Teina. Both Teina and Mauta are buried by that high-pointed stone, but the king was killed at sea by a turtle." The old man laughed. "They say that every night after Mauta's death, Teina would sit by the beach at Yato, and sing:

"I will wait for you a year,
And then half a year, my husband.

But she didn't. One night one of the bucks from Yato came down to hear her sing, and it turned out that she didn't wait nearly so long as she promised she would.

"Teina's bones are in the grave in front of you." (I heard the *glug-glug* of the rum bottle; then it was passed to me.) "You can still hear her of a night when the moon rises, singing about how she'll wait a year and a half a year for her husband. She was a shameless trollop!"

A diffused light like a phosphorescent mist seemed to steal across the cemetery. I could again see old William's face and the gravestones stood out sharply. My heart pumped double-time for a moment; then I realized what had happened: the moon was rising.

The old heathen up-ended the rum bottle, threw it aside, and spread out his arms in a wide gesture.

"My father lies over there on the sea side of the graveyard," he said. "He's under that tall square stone. He was a fathom and six fingers high, and he weighed three hundred and eighty-five pounds on Captain Hayes's scales. My mother's grave is the next one, and then the graves of my six brothers and sisters."

Another group of phantom figures, but less distinct than the rest, seemed to rise from the ground as though old William had conjured them up; but in a moment they dissolved in the light of the rising moon.

"Do you see that blank space to the right? That's for Mama and me."

Suddenly he grasped me by the shoulder, put his face close to mine, and gazed into my eyes with a leering, drunken smile.

"But there's plenty of room for three, Ropati! We'll leave a place for you. Carramba!" he shouted. "I will now compose the rest of your death chant!"